Capital Allocation and Value Creation

Torbjörn Arenbo

Capital Allocation and Value Creation

A Market-Based Framework for Executives

palgrave
macmillan

Torbjörn Arenbo
Malmö, Sweden

ISBN 978-3-031-47047-9 ISBN 978-3-031-47048-6 (eBook)
https://doi.org/10.1007/978-3-031-47048-6

This Palgrave Macmillan imprint is published by the registered company Springer Nature Switzerland AG
The registered company address is: Gewerbestrasse 11, 6330 Cham, Switzerland

Paper in this product is recyclable.

Acknowledgements

This book delves into the concept of capital allocation—how companies strategically deploy their cash flow to generate value. It draws upon and reflects the work my team and I have developed over the past ten years. I have been incredibly fortunate to collaborate with numerous outstanding colleagues and have gained valuable insights from countless conversations with clients. In that context, I would like to extend a special thank you to NIBE's CEO Gerteric Lindquist and CFO Hans Backman, who have contributed to the content of the book by sharing their insightful thoughts on making acquisitions. Their influence, along with that of Michael Mauboussin and Dan Callahan at Morgan Stanley, who introduced me to a fresh perspective on capital allocation, has contributed to shaping the ideas and thoughts presented in this book.

I am deeply grateful to all the exceptional individuals at Danske Bank who have worked closely with me in the corporate banking department. I would like to extend a special thanks to Peter Trigarszky and Oskar Haglund, my close colleagues for the past 9 years. Their invaluable contributions have been instrumental in shaping much of the ideas and content reflected in this book. Additionally, Oskar has been an invaluable resource throughout the practical preparation of this book, and I owe its completion to his exceptional support.

I am also deeply grateful to Joacim Nässén, my supervisor at Danske Bank, for his belief in, and support of, this project.

Thanks also go to both present and former colleagues who have taken the time to read and provide feedback on the draft of this book. Among them, I am especially thankful to my former colleague from Copenhagen, John Bäckman, and my mentor from Lund University, Per Frennberg, both of whom have influenced and inspired the ideas presented here.

Additionally, I would like to extend my gratitude to Stefan Lind, Senior Banker at Danske Bank, Dan Christiernsson, portfolio manager at Alecta, and Magnus Jonasson, Head of asset allocation at AMF, for their valuable insights and contributions.

I am also very grateful to my father-in-law, Christer Jönsson, professor emeritus at Lund University, for editing the manuscript.

Lastly, I wish to express my appreciation to my wonderful wife, Lena, and my children, Lukas and Elsa, for their patience and support throughout the writing process of this book.

Contents

Abbreviations

BCG	Boston Consulting Group
BIS	Bank for International Settlements
CAGR	Compound Annual Growth Rate
CAPE	Cyclically Adjusted Price Earnings
CAPM	Capital Asset Pricing Model
CEO	Chief Executive Officer
CFO	Cash Flow from Operations
CFO	Chief Financial Officer
COO	Chief Operating Officer
DCF	Discounted Cash Flow Model
DDM	Dividend Discount Model
EBIT	Earnings Before Interest and Tax
EBITA	Earnings Before Interest, Tax, and Amortization
EBITDA	Earnings Before Interest, Tax, Depreciation, and Amortization
ECB	European Central Bank
EPS	Earnings Per Share
EV	Enterprise Value
FCF	Free Cash Flow
GDP	Gross Domestic Product
GFC	Global Financial Crises
GW	Goodwill
IPO	Initial Public Offering
KPI	Key Performance Indicator
M&A	Mergers and Acquisitions
NOPAT	Net Operating Profit after Tax
NPV	Net Present Value

NWC	Net Working Capital
P/E	Price-to-Earnings
PPE	Property, Plant, and Equipment
R&D	Research and Development
RCF	Revolving Credit Facility
ROCE	Return on Capital Employed
ROE	Return on Equity
ROIC	Return on Invested Capital
SBB	Share Buyback
TSR	Total Shareholder Return
WACC	Weighted Average Cost of Capital

List of Figures

CHAPTER 1

Introduction

In order to run a company efficiently, it is not sufficient to simply be a competent businessperson. One must also possess the skills of a knowledgeable investor. The management must determine where to invest capital given the diverse range of investment options available, such as mergers and acquisitions (M&A), dividends, share repurchase programmes, and organic growth opportunities.

By adopting a practical, market-oriented approach to capital allocation, we aim to shed light on the complex issue of cash flow deployment and the creation of shareholder value. The book provides a useful analytical framework for corporate executives to consider when allocating capital, along with empirical findings from peer-group studies and company case studies.

The book will help you answer questions like:

- What are the primary factors that drive your company's shareholder value? And are they aligned with the strategy the company is pursuing?
- What are the key dynamics and trade-offs between return on investments (ROIC), growth, and earnings quality?
- What are the current market expectations embedded in the stock price?

T. Arenbo, *Capital Allocation and Value Creation*,
https://doi.org/10.1007/978-3-031-47048-6_1

- Given the capital allocation priorities, what does an "optimal" capital structure look like?
- How do you set, and in turn communicate, the capital allocation and funding priorities?

To Master Capital Allocation, You Have to Think Like an Investor

The art and science of capital allocation are not taught at the universities. In order to learn and master this subject you have to find and put together the pieces yourself. One crucial ingredient to successful capital allocation is to think and act like an investor. That typically includes having an analytical mind-set with a clear and objective stance towards risk and reward. And maybe that is one reason why so many corporate executives struggle to reach the required skill set when it comes to capital allocation. Research conducted on CEOs' personality traits shows a high score for characters like execution ability, charisma, and strategic ability. However, compared to the larger peer group consisting of, for example, CFOs and COOs, they score lower on typical "investor traits" like analytical ability and attention to detail. See Kaplan and Sorensen (2020) and Graham et al. (2013).

It does, however, not explain the surprisingly limited attention the capital allocation as a subject gets compared to other financial and managerial topics. Except for Warren Buffet and Charlie Munger and the attention William Thorndike received for his book "Outsiders", not many books have made it to a broader audience. See Thorndike (2012).

But as Warren Buffet puts it: "*Most bosses rise to the top because they have excelled in an area such as marketing, production, engineering, administration or, sometimes, institutional politics. Once they become CEOs, they face new responsibilities. They now must make capital allocation decisions, a critical job that they may have never tackled and that is not easily mastered. In the end, plenty of unintelligent capital allocation takes place in corporate America. That's why you hear so much about "restructuring."*" Buffet (1987).

What stands out in Thorndike's "Outsiders" is how the eight reviewed CEOs manage to think as long-term owners with a strong focus on how each dollar best can be put into use. In several of the eight cases, the CEOs had a very close and long-lasting relation with the COO, who was given a large responsibility for the day-to-day operations of the firm, allowing the CEO to focus on allocating capital and resources.

The CEO's skills as a capital allocator will evidently be one of the top differentiating drivers for the value creation over the longer term. A fact that will become evident in this book.

The Corporate "Eco-System"

The cash flow a company generates can, broadly speaking, be deployed in two different ways. Either it is used to grow the business, organically or through acquisitions, or it is returned to investors through dividends, share buybacks, or amortization of debt (Fig. 1.1).

One of the big challenges with capital allocation is how to compare different cash flow deployment alternatives with each other. In practice, it means being able to adequately handle questions like:

- How can we ensure that the capital allocation decisions are aligned with the long-term profitability and growth targets?
- How should the CEO allocate resources to different business units displaying varying prospects for growth and profitability?
- What criteria should be used to evaluate potential acquisition targets or investment opportunities?
- What should the balance look like between investing in the core business versus exploring new growth opportunities?
- A company has excess cash to return to shareholders but the share price trades at a historically low multiple. Should the company increase the ordinary dividend, pay out an extra dividend, or start buying back shares?
- A company has recently acquired another business, partially funded by issuing new shares. Despite the recent stock issuance, should the company still pay the regular dividend to its shareholders?
- The debt to enterprise value ratio for a company is indicating a fragile financial position. What would a cost–benefit analysis of issuing new shares look like?

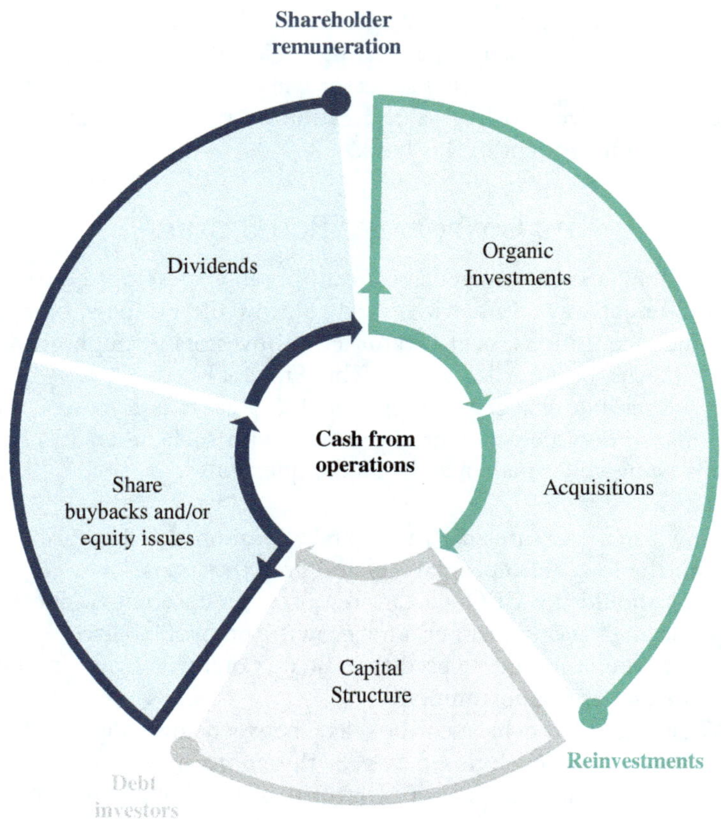

Fig. 1.1 The corporate "eco-system"

Using the Market for Guidance

The financial market is a rich source of information that can provide guidance to the capital allocation process. According to financial theory, value creation is determined by a company's return on investment capital (ROIC), growth, and cost of capital. However, some may question the relationship between valuation theory and market prices, given the apparent high volatility in the stock market.

However, when we and others compare the theoretical value drivers with empirical data, we find a strong correlation between the performance drivers and stock market valuation, particularly over the long run. This correlation highlights the valuable insights that the market can provide to capital allocators.

In fact, an effective capital allocation process should not only rely on sound theory but also leverage the valuable information available in the market. Capital allocators with profound understanding of the market can greatly impact value creation for their companies.

This book takes a practical approach to help corporate executives understand how to use the information provided by the market as input in their capital allocation process. We will discuss how to analyze market data and use it to evaluate potential investment opportunities, and how to balance theoretical frameworks with real-world market insights. By the end of this book, readers will have a solid understanding of how to optimize their capital allocation decisions using the market as a powerful tool.

The Structure of the Book

The book is structured in four parts. The first three parts will in turn focus on various aspects of value creation, the cash flow deployment alternatives, and the insights gained by being able to read the market and think like an investor. The fourth and final part is where the framework comes together.

In **Part I**, comprising three chapters, we begin by introducing a theoretical framework for assessing and analyzing value creation. The aim is to gain a better understanding of the balance and interplay between ROIC, growth, and the cost of capital. We then supplement the analytical framework by adopting a market-based approach to shed light on the delicate question of capital allocation and shareholder value creation. Finally, in Part I, we discuss how management could consider the link between earnings quality and shareholder value creation.

Moving on to **Part II**, consisting of five chapters, we explore the various alternatives for capital allocation and cash flow deployment available to management. We initiate the discussion by focusing on a topic of high priority on many managers' agendas: Mergers and Acquisitions (M&As). We then proceed to review different aspects of business downsizing, such as divestment or spinning off a business unit. Additionally, we delve into the means by which capital can be returned to investors through dividends and share buybacks. Part II concludes by highlighting several aspects related to establishing the desired risk level for the capital structure and funding.

Part III, consisting of three chapters, starts by providing a macroeconomic background and introducing how investor preferences may vary across different financial policy regimes. Furthermore, we explore how corporate managers can benefit from adopting an "investor mindset" when allocating capital. Specifically, we emphasize three typical investor skills: developing a well-defined risk-reward mind-set, employing a rule-based approach to investing, and utilizing various techniques for scenario modelling. Part III concludes with an empirical study focused on how a company can emerge as a winner from a recession.

Finally, in **Part IV**, we tie the first three parts of the book together in a capital allocation framework. We start by discussing financial targets and provide guidance on how to set them in accordance to the company's most important value drivers. We then present a case study of what a markets-based capital allocation process could look like. The summary chapter of the book contains a comprehensive three-step capital allocation framework.

Whether you are a business leader, financial analyst, or investor, this book will provide you with an easy-to-use framework for capital allocation as well as give you better insights to the workings of the financial markets, with the ultimate goal to drive value creation.

References

Buffet WE (1987) Letter to Shareholders. Berkshire Hathaway Annual Report.

Graham JR, Harvey CR, Puri M (2013) Managerial Attitudes and Corporate Actions. Journal of Financial Economics 109:103–121.

Kaplan SN, Sorensen M (2020) Are CFOs Different? Published online. https://papers.ssrn.com/sol3/papers.cfm?abstract_id=2747691.

Thorndike WN (2012) The Outsiders: Eight Unconventional CEOs and Their Radically Rational Blueprint for Success. Harvard Business School Publishing.

PART I

The Value Drivers That Matters

In the first part of this book, we will present a powerful framework for value creation based on three value drivers: Return on Invested Capital (ROIC), growth, and cost of capital. We have chosen to use a set-up based on ROIC rather than a Discounted Cash Flow (DCF) model for pedagogical reasons. However, the two models are linked, and with correctly defined terms, they will yield the same results.

The first step business leaders must take on their journey to create more value is to get the capital allocation priorities right. The specific strategy to adopt and the appropriate value creation lever to pull can vary greatly from one company to another. In capital allocation, unfortunately, "one size fits all" does not apply. Another layer of complexity is added by the fact that the relationship between the value drivers is non-linear. This makes it hard to understand the valuation "trade-offs" between ROIC, growth, and cost of capital intuitively.

As a tool to better understand value creation, we will introduce a Total Shareholder Return (TSR) model. The TSR model allows managers to evaluate the overall performance of a company's stock over a given period of time. By analyzing the different factors that influence TSR, managers can gain important insights into what drives the market value of the company. We highlight how the TSR framework can be used in practice by conducting a large peer-group study as well as through two in-depth case studies.

We conclude part one by shedding some extra light on the sometimes overlooked role that earnings quality plays in the valuation process. Earnings quality is tightly linked to valuation through its strong correlation with the cost of capital. The last two decades have been characterized by low nominal growth, which has led many managers to prioritize growth as a top strategic priority. However, for a large proportion of companies, increased profitability and margin stability would bring much greater reward in terms of shareholder value than aiming for higher growth. A turn to a more inflationary environment would further highlight the significance of earnings quality as a crucial value driver going forward.

CHAPTER 2

Value Creation—The Theoretical Foundation

Without a sufficient understanding of the theoretical building blocks of value creation, it becomes challenging to make informed decisions regarding capital allocation. Therefore, in this chapter, we start by very briefly describing what roles return on invested capital (ROIC), growth, and cost of capital play in the value creation framework as well as highlight the interaction between them.

The Three Drivers of Value—Profitability, Growth, and Cost of Capital

What do the financial markets really care about when it comes to value creation? According to corporate finance theory, companies create value by generating cash flows, which are discounted by the cost of capital. While numerous valuation models exist, we prefer, for pedagogical reasons, the key value driver model, which explicitly links value creation to ROIC, growth, and cost of capital.

In brief, it can be described as depicted in Fig. 2.1.[1]

[1] For an in-depth explanation of the fundamental principles of value creation, see, for example, Chapter 3 in "Valuation" by McKinsey & Company et al. (2020).

T. Arenbo, *Capital Allocation and Value Creation*,
https://doi.org/10.1007/978-3-031-47048-6_2

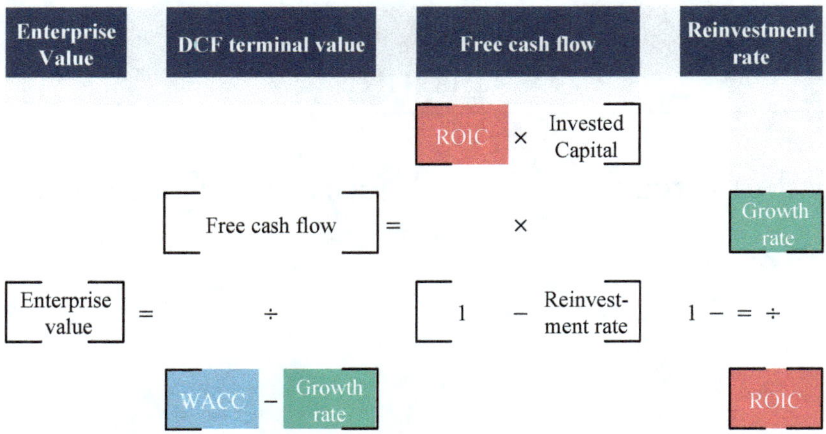

Fig. 2.1 How the enterprise value can be linked to the three value drivers

A company has to earn above its cost of capital to create value. The total amount of value a company can create over time is determined by a company's ROIC versus cost of capital spread, its revenue growth, and its capacity to sustainably keep these two drivers of value high over long periods of time.[2]

In this equation, you can see why ROIC matters so much. If you want to grow, it will cost you a part of today's free cash flow. The higher your ROIC, the "cheaper" your growth is in the sense that you still can generate high levels of cash flow today.[3]

[2] There are many measurements of profitability. Return on equity (ROE), return on assets (ROA) and return on capital employed (ROCE) to mention a few. The theory behind value creation, the research done on stock market performance, and the valuation professionals in the real world quite unanimously suggest that ROIC is the preferred measure to use.

[3] Even though the formula is designed for calculating terminal value, it is our preferred way of thinking about value creation since it gives a good sense of the key drivers of value.

Return on Invested Capital

Since the global financial crisis (GFC), investors have had a strong focus on finding growth companies. However, growth is not for everyone, and it seems that some corporations may have forgotten the importance of the return on capital in creating value. When the dust settles after the growth phase, companies with a low or negative ROIC spread will find that very little or no value has been created. Long-term investors allocate a significant portion of their resources to investigating the size and sustainability of a company's excess returns. A CEO should always be capable of explaining to the market where and why their company is expected to create value by generating returns above the cost of capital. This serves as the analytical starting point for any value investor. Therefore, we begin this chapter with a review of various aspects of ROIC.

A Basic Understanding of ROIC

In the corporate world, the focus on profitability sometimes relies too heavily on various margin measures. However, ROIC is a preferred measure to use when analyzing value creation because it provides an indication of how well a company is generating profits relative to the amount of capital it has invested in its business.

ROIC is based on Net Operating Profit After Taxes (NOPAT), which aims to represent the normal unlevered profit generated from a company's core operations after tax. By excluding any financing or investment activities, ROIC provides a clearer picture of the company's ability to generate profit from its business activities.

The formula for calculating ROIC is:

$$\text{Net Operating Profit After Taxes (NOPAT)/Invested Capital}$$

To calculate **NOPAT**, you can begin with the company's operating profit before amortizations but after depreciations, and then adjust for cash taxes. By using earnings before interest, tax, and amortization (EBITA), adjusted for capitalized development costs, as the starting point for calculating NOPAT, you can obtain a more accurate picture of the company's profitability. To adjust for taxes, multiply the company's operating profit by its stated tax rate.

Once you have the NOPAT figure, you can calculate invested capital, which represents the amount of money the company has invested in its business. Invested capital can be calculated from both the asset side and the liability side of the balance sheet. Both methods have their pros and cons, but we prefer to calculate ROIC using the asset side approach as it provides a solid foundation for analyzing asset efficiency.

The asset side (or operating) approach to calculating invested capital begins by identifying operating assets directly involved in the company's operations, such as property, plant, and equipment (PPE), acquired intangibles, goodwill, inventory, and accounts receivable. Non-operating assets that are not essential to the company's ongoing business operations, such as excess cash, marketable securities, and non-core holdings, are then excluded. Finally, non-interest bearing operating liabilities, such as accounts payable, are removed.

In its simplest form, the formula for calculating invested capital using the operating approach can be represented as:

$$\text{Invested Capital} = \text{PPE} + \text{Intangibles} + \text{Goodwill} + \text{Net Working Capital}$$

ROIC and Competitive Advantage

At the very heart of value creation lies the ability to achieve a durable competitive advantage. Or as Warren Buffet put it, "*A truly great business must have an enduring 'moat' that protects excellent returns on invested capital*". Thus, one of the most important task for the CEO is to make excess returns as sustainable as possible.

However, in a free-market setting, competitive forces tend to bring the return on invested capital closer to the cost of capital. Additionally, any external factors affecting short to medium-term performance will balance out over the long term. That being said, different industries revert to the mean at different rates, and large variations in ROIC can exist within industries. As our peer studies in the next chapter will demonstrate, strategy and capital allocation definitely have an important role to play.

There are numerous frameworks that business leaders and investors can use to assess a firm's potential to maintain a competitive position and durable ROIC spread. However, as industry analysis and business strategy to a large extent are outside the scope of this book, we confine ourselves to the analysis provided by splitting up the ROIC in a margin component and an asset turnover component.[4]

In that way, we can gain a better understanding of how a company attempts to create value. The competitive advantage might, for example, be achieved through a ***differentiation strategy***, which typically manifests itself as a higher operating margin. A competitive advantage might also be attained through a *cost leadership strategy*, which can be indicated by a higher asset turnover.[5]

Differentiation Versus Cost Leadership Strategies

According to Porter (1980), a company can compete by offering superior non-price benefits such as a great brand, an exciting style, or excellent functionality; or it can try to attract customers with lower prices. The choice between a price differentiation strategy and a cost leadership strategy depends on various factors, including the market dynamics, competitive landscape, target customers, and the company's capabilities. Both strategies have their advantages and can be effective in different situations.

In an ambitious study, Raynor and Ahmed (2013) analyzed data on more than 25,000 companies spanning forty-five years, trying to answer the question of whether it is better to keep price down or to invest in creating value that commands a higher price.

They reach the conclusion that really outstanding performance more often is generated by greater value and not by lower price. They claim that companies seeking sustained, exceptional profitability should try to build competitive positions, or "moats", by greater differentiation through features like brand, style, or reliability. We will revert to ROIC as a value driver on many occasions throughout this book, not least in our case studies. And on a more anecdotal note, Raynor and Ahmed's conclusions seem to align well with our case study findings.

[4] ROIC = (NOPAT/Sales) × (Sales/Invested capital) where the first term expresses the NOPAT-margin and the second term expresses the capital turnover ratio.

[5] The Porter model is one of the more popular models used when it comes to industry and strategy analysis. Porter argues that the attractiveness of an industry can be analyzed by looking at five competitive forces: (1) The intensity of rivalry among industry incumbents (2), the bargaining power of suppliers, (3) the bargaining power of buyers, (4) the threat of entry of new firms, and (5) the availability of substitute products. For further reading we recommend Magretta (2012).

Growth

We will now look into how the value framework can improve the capital allocation process for corporate executives by examining the value trade-offs between ROIC and growth. This relationship is not always intuitive, but, as previously stated, value creation starts with ROIC. Once your ROIC is high enough, growth becomes more and more valuable.

Balancing Profitability and Growth in the Valuation Framework

In Fig. 2.2, we aim to illustrate the relationship between ROIC and growth by depicting an "iso-value" curve. The curve demonstrates the trade-off between ROIC and growth when the terminal ROIC versus cost of capital spread approaches zero. Our focus is on the slope of the curve. For a company with a high ROIC versus cost of capital spread, the trade-off line is very flat, indicating that changes in growth compared to changes in ROIC can be advantageous. Conversely, for a company with a ROIC close to the cost of capital, the reverse relationship holds true. This steep part of the trade-off curve is where most of our peer-group companies are situated. For example, in our defined set-up, a company with a ROIC versus cost of capital spread of 3%-points would experience roughly the same increase in value from a 1%-point increase in ROIC as from a 5%-point increase in sales growth.

The "iso-value" line clearly shows that there is no one solution for all companies, but rather that the starting point of the trade-off begins with assessing the ROIC versus cost of capital spread. The non-linear relationship makes it hard to understand these valuation trade-offs intuitively. But if you do the math using a DCF model, you would probably be surprised to see how much more value an increase in ROIC will bring compared to increased growth. Based on our experience, we believe that, merely by understanding the message of Fig. 2.2, a lot of poor capital allocation decisions could be avoided.

Given that growth has been a popular trend among investors for some time, it is not surprising to observe that the common mistakes in the past two decades have involved companies with too low a return on invested capital trying to achieve growth at an excessive cost.

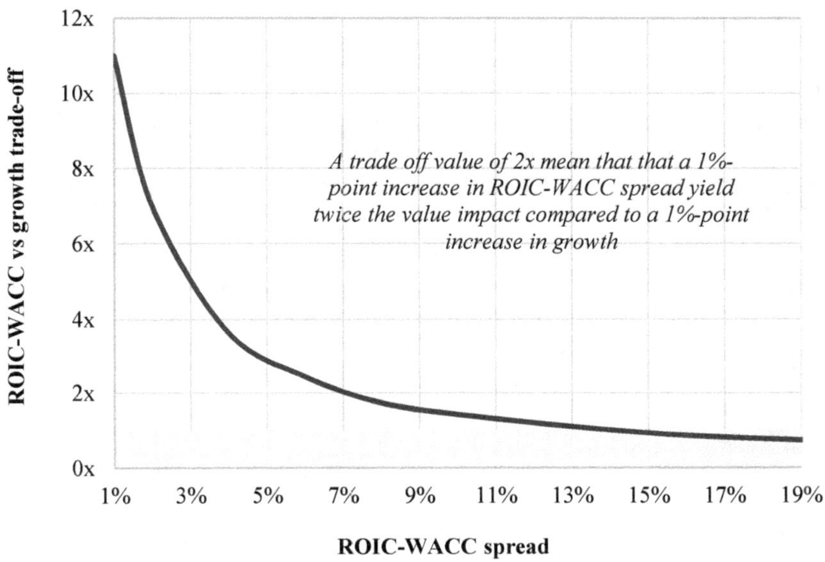

Fig. 2.2 Balancing profitability and growth in an "iso-value" curve

Balancing Profitability and Growth in Real Life

When looking at the strategic goals of a vast majority of companies, one might get the impression that growth is the primary factor in determining shareholder return and essential for creating above-average long-term value. However, as we will show empirically later in the book, it is crucial to consider both the source and the cost of growth, as they can have significant impacts on value creation.

Growth can be value destroying for various reasons. For instance, as Fig. 2.2 tried to illustrate, organic growth may come at an excessive cost, resulting in ROIC dilution. Companies often aim to grow by targeting the same market without a differentiated competitive strategy. Acquired growth can also lead to overpayment for potential synergies, benefiting the seller more than the acquiring company. Additionally, growth initiatives can change the risk profile, leading to lower earnings quality and a higher cost of capital. These are all topics we will get back to later in the book.

Therefore, growth is closely connected to the other fundamental value drivers and must be evaluated in that context. Studies have indicated that for companies with a high return spread, the market reacts positively to unexpected increases in capital expenditures. On the other hand, unexpected decreases in capital expenditures result in a negative response from the market. See McConnell and Muscarella (1985) and Chung et al. (1998).

Another, and sometimes overlooked aspect of growth, is how the specific supply dynamics in an industry look like. In Chancellor's (2015) book "Capital Returns: Investing Through the Capital Cycle", we learn more about how a long-term investor can look at supply-side dynamics and their effects on growth and margins. He claims that a high current profitability often leads to overconfidence among managers, which in turn loosens capital discipline in an industry. Too high a focus on short-term EPS growth eventually makes the capital cycle turn down as excess capacity becomes apparent. Chancellor outlines four key factors that drive what he describes as the "capital cycle anomaly": competition neglect, base rate neglect, narrow framing, and extrapolation.

Chancellor's investor-based arguments tally well with our empirical findings presented in the next chapter as well as with a broader set of academic literature.

As a final remark about growth, we can conclude that it is, just like ROIC, a mean-reverting variable. However, history tells us that growth tends to mean-revert at a higher rate than ROIC does. See, for example, McKinsey (2006). This is partly because most product markets have natural life cycles. Partly it is a pure mathematical consequence of getting bigger.

Cost of Capital

The third pillar of value creation, the cost of capital, is an important but elusive factor in the capital allocation puzzle. The cost of capital serves as the "alternative cost anchor" against which all capital allocation decisions should be compared.[6] But even so, many corporate executives, as well

[6] We like to think about the cost of capital, or the investors required return, as the opportunity cost if the investor were to invest the money in other assets with comparable risk. Unless cash flow is going to its best and highest returning use, it is underperforming relative to its opportunity cost.

as boards, lack the basic knowledge around (and sometimes interest in) the subject. To some extent, this is understandable. After all, the cost of capital is a more or less fixed variable for a company, at least in the short term. The fact that it is not directly visible only adds to the complexity of the issue. Nonetheless, there are several good reasons why it is important to be familiar with the basics of this topic.

Earnings Quality as a Proxy for the Cost of Capital

We believe that the most important way to think about cost of capital is through the lens of earnings quality. The link between earnings quality and the cost of capital is a critical consideration for investors and managers when assessing the risk profile of a company. There are several indicators of earnings quality, including the consistency, predictability, and transparency of a company's earnings. Companies that, for example, display a high degree of pricing power and margin stability are often rewarded with a lower cost of capital which, in turn, boosts the valuation of the firm. The link between earnings quality and cost of capital, and its effect on valuation, has, in our opinion, received too little attention from the corporate as well as the academic world.

A market environment with high and volatile inflation will to a larger extent differentiate between high and low volatility cash flow streams. And with the overall scarcity of low-risk assets, investors have increasingly started to favour stable-yielding equities. As a result, factors such as improved margins and cash flow stability help companies increase their market value by reducing their cost of capital. For companies with long cash flow durations, a lower discount rate can result in a substantial increase in their market value. This is evident from the drastic revaluations of forest holding companies such as Holmen and SCA in the mid-2010s. They saw their cost of capital reduced by half, leading to an increase in their price-to-sales ratio from 1.4× to 3.4× in just a few years. We will return to this topic in Chapter 4, where we will make an in-depth review of the role earnings quality plays in the value creation process.

CFOs Prefer Using the Capital Asset Pricing Model (CAPM)

When CFOs are asked about how they determine the firm's cost of equity, their answer reveals a heavy reliance on the CAPM. In the 2022 Duke CFO survey, 83% of large firms always or almost always use CAPM to estimate their firm's cost of equity. Second in popularity, which 69% of respondents claim to use, is the multi-factor model. Third in ranking comes the use of historical averages of the cost of equity, and only fourth in order is asking the investors about their expectations (30% of respondents). Deriving the cost of capital from implied market return expectations ranks even lower and is used by only 17% of the large firms. See Graham (2022).

Why Using CAPM and WACC Could Lead You "Precisely Wrong" Rather Than "Roughly Right"

Maybe it should not come as a surprise to find out about the popularity of using CAPM. If you open any textbook on the subject of the cost of capital, the first reference you will likely find is to the Capital Asset Pricing Model (CAPM) and the Weighted Average Cost of Capital (WACC). You will also find numerous chapters covering the calculation and input factors such as the risk-free rate, equity risk premium, and unlevered beta. Although WACC is a nice and easy-to-use theoretical construct, we are not convinced of its practical usefulness. There are several reasons for our scepticism.

- First, there has been too much uncertainty surrounding the duration of low interest rates for investors to fully lower their return requirements. As a result, we have seen an arbitrary interest rate "rebound" factor implemented into cost of capital calculations.[7]
- Second, the inputs used to calculate the cost of equity are based on past stock price volatility, while investing is a forward-looking activity. Business risk is not constant over time.[8]
- Third, academic research has shown a large variation in companies' choices for the risk-free rate, beta, and the equity market risk premium, making the CAPM model arbitrary and inconsistent.
- Finally, in our experience, the relationship between the cost of equity and leverage in many industries is more or less constant, up to a

[7] Japan can be used as a reference. The country has had low interest rates for very long yet been reluctant to lower the cost of capital.

[8] The pandemic, for example, did not affect the economy the same way as the global financial crisis did.

certain point. When a company is deemed to be at risk of financial distress, the cost of equity increases sharply, making the cost of equity look more like a hockey stick than a smooth upward-sloping line.[9]

One of the biggest risks with using the WACC construct is that you may end up being "precisely wrong" rather than "roughly right". And when it comes to cost of capital, "roughly right" will do just fine! Here is how we think about "points of reference" in order to get it "roughly right".

The Market-Implied Cost of Capital

This methodology uses the market information and a DCF or DDM model in order to extract the implicit discount rates for a specific company or market. This is the methodology the well renowned academic Aswath Damodaran uses (Damodaran 2023). The calculations he has made for S&P500 between 2008 and 2022 have, despite falling interest rates, resulted in relatively stable expected returns around 7.5–8.0%.

The European Central Bank (ECB) has conducted similar computations using a three-stage dividend discount model for the Eurozone. Their results as well indicate that the cost of equity has been relatively stable, fluctuating between 7 and 9% since 2005. See ECB (2018).

Asking the Market Participants

This is a survey based methodology where different kinds of market participants are asked about the market risk premium. For the Nordic markets, we refer to a survey conducted by PwC (2022), which demonstrates the same negative correlation between interest rates and equity risk premium as the market-implied cost of capital methodology. From 2000 until the financial crisis, the equity market risk premium averaged 4.5%, but for 2021–2022, the figure has significantly increased to above 6.5%. The rise in risk premiums compensates for the declining interest rates, resulting in a relatively stable cost of equity.

[9] Except for a few very stable sectors, equity investors do not seem to be overly concerned about leverage and its effect on the overall cost of capital as long as the perception of financial stability prevails.

The Cost of Capital for Your Company

A third and more direct way of getting to know your cost of capital is to ask your long-term owners about their required return expectations. They will probably not give you a number but their response might provide some clues about how they think about the "opportunity cost" of the capital invested in your company.

We generally use the market-implied cost of capital methodology for individual companies, as well as for a market or index. We use a DCF model in order to extract the implicit cost of capital. But as the DCF model is infamously known for its sensitivity to the input chosen, be especially aware of a few things when doing the calculations.

- Make sure not to underestimate the capex needs required to achieve the estimated growth. You should examine the relationship between ROIC, margins, and capex. If the margins are stable, but the ROIC increases, it could indicate that the capex estimates are too low. Many companies with "normal" growth rate can be expected to have an average long-term capex to depreciation ratio of 1.2–1.4×. However, large variations between sectors exist.
- When locking the model in the steady state period, think in terms of ROIC and not margin. ROIC is a mean-reverting variable, and it is crucial to have a realistic assumption about the long-term ROIC versus cost of capital spread.
- Think in terms of cost of capital on an enterprise value level—do not spend too much time trying to estimate the equity and debt components separately. We believe it is sufficient to assume a normalized leverage ratio and reasonable levels of the borrowing costs.

Cost of Capital Over Time and Across Sectors

Over the years, we have conducted numerous market-implied cost of capital calculations and most companies fall within the range of 7–9%. In some stable cash flow generating sectors, such as the telecom industry, we have observed discount rates as low as 5–6%. Meanwhile, in cyclical industries, some companies can have rates exceeding 10%. However, for larger companies, a reasonable starting point for cost of capital discussions would be around 7–8%.

As a final verification of whether managers may have altered the required return on investments, we take a closer look at the development of corporate profitability. Ideally, over time, you would expect a positive correlation between cost of capital and return on invested capital. But when we examine a large European sample of companies between 1999 and 2020, we do not see a clear correlation between declining interest rates and reduced profitability. On average for the group, return on investments appears to have decreased only slightly. However, for three out of the ten sectors, there are clear signs of falling returns, namely for the real estate, energy, and utility sectors.

To summarize, the cost of capital, for most sectors, remains relatively stable over time and does not seem to be significantly impacted by changes in interest rates. Corporations have a widespread reluctance to increase leverage and decrease the hurdle rates indicated by the secular trend of decreasing interest rates. This is probably for good reasons. There is limited evidence that investors have actually lowered their required returns on a broader scale. For instance, a company that invests at a too low hurdle rate would run the risk of locking in low returns for a prolonged period. Furthermore, the threat of financial distress that increased leverage brings and the high costs associated with it are a concern for many companies.

How to Use and Interpret Valuation Multiples

We devote the last part of this chapter to a discussion about multiples. A corporate executive who wants to better understand valuation needs to be able to decipher multiples, as a very large part of equity research reports as well as acquisition valuations are based upon a multiple. In our experience, however, a lot of the corporate executives struggle when trying to interpret these numbers to their full capacity. And as the use of multiples is full of potential pitfalls, this could lead to poor capital allocation decisions. The good news is that some of the most commonly used multiples are closely related to the fundamental value drivers presented earlier in this chapter. First and foremost, a valuation multiple is nothing more than a shorthand for a discounted cash flow (DCF)-based valuation method.

Which Valuation Multiple Should You Consider?

When it comes to valuation multiples, there are numerous options to choose from. However, we have limited the list to a few that can be derived from a DCF model.[10]

Price to Earnings (P/E)
The P/E ratio is a popular multiple among financial investors, but it has two significant flaws. Firstly, as it is a stock measure and not an enterprise value measure, it ignores the impact of different capital structures. Secondly, it is based on net earnings and often includes non-operating items, such as restructuring charges and write-offs, which can skew the results.

Enterprise Value to EBITDA (EV/EBITDA)
This ratio is frequently used as a rough measure of cash flow, particularly by lenders. However, it overlooks the capital intensity of a business and the significant differences in reinvestment needs among various sectors. EBITDA is not a recognized accounting term and is often reported on an adjusted basis, where great accounting liberties sometimes have been taken.

Enterprise Value to Operating Earnings (EV/EBIT or EV/EBITA)
Our preferred multiple to use is the Enterprise Value to Earnings Before Interest, Taxes and Amortization (EV/EBITA). The difference between EBIT and EBITA is the amortization of intangible assets, such as acquired brands, customers, and capitalized research and development expenses. Unlike the depreciation of physical assets, these are mostly non-cash expenses, as the replacement costs have already been accounted for in the cost of goods sold. However, be aware that when it comes to the capitalized research and development (R&D) expenses, these often resemble those of ordinary depreciations.

Additionally, we prefer to use multiples based on two to three years of forecasted profits rather than historical profits, because we believe that

[10] Other commonly used multiples like Price-to-book and Price-to-capital, are not linked to the fundamental value formulas the same way as the multiples we have chosen above.

it better reflects investors' normalized view of earnings and excludes any distorting one-off items.

In terms of the three value drivers, the EV/EBITA multiple can be expressed as follows:

$$\text{EV/EBITA} = (\text{ROIC-growth})/(\text{ROIC} \times (\text{WACC-growth})) \times (1 - \text{tax rate})$$

Benefits of Understanding Valuation Multiples

Investors typically use multiples when comparing the valuations of companies within a sector. From a corporate perspective, several benefits of understanding the ins and outs of multiples come to mind. For one, it can help managers understand why companies in the same sector trade at different multiples. It is also a simple and powerful tool when trying to determine which long-term expectations are embedded in the share price.

For instance, this type of analysis is relevant when companies that are rewarded with a high multiple due to high growth expectations try to answer questions such as:

- How much growth is required to justify the current multiple?
- And, as a result, how much capital would be needed to achieve that growth?
- Would acquiring a company valued at a higher multiple than my own be value destroying?

Moreover, managers that understand how to interpret their own multiples can benefit when it comes to investor relations. They can better explain factors influencing the company's valuation and address potential gaps between the market's perception of the value drivers and their own. This can be the case, not least when it comes to how the perception of risk influences valuation. However, it will also be an advantage if management can confidently articulate and defend their valuation during M&A negotiations.

Limitations and Common Pitfalls Using Valuation Multiples

As previously mentioned, it is crucial to understand that multiples are a simplified representation of a complex valuation process. As such, the use of valuation multiples comes with some limitations. They may for instance overlook market sentiment and earnings cyclicality as well as accounting differences between companies.

Despite their widespread use as a valuation tool for target companies, it is crucial to keep focus on the key factors that drive value, i.e. profitability, growth, and cost of capital. Without a proper analysis of these value drivers, it is not possible to determine, for example, whether an acquisition with a "negative multiple spread" would be value dilutive.

When considering multiples in the context of acquisitions, there are several factors that deserve extra attention. Beyond the more obvious distortions like cyclical earnings and one-time events, there may be other less obvious factors to look out for.

- If a company is rewarded with a high multiple thanks to high growth expectations, make sure not to underestimate the capital required to achieve that growth. History often provides a good guidance. Look at the capex to sales ratio over time and pay special attention to the split between organic and acquired growth.
- If a company is rewarded with a high multiple thanks to a high ROIC level, make sure to have reasonable expectations about the duration of the excess profitability. Remember that ROIC tends to be a mean-reverting variable.
- Using the EV/EBITA multiple, pay extra attention to the extent to which companies make use of the possibility to capitalize R&D. It can vary both over time as well as across companies and can make comparisons more difficult.

Conclusions

The first step business leaders must take on their journey to create more value is to get the capital allocation priorities right. The specific strategy to adopt and the appropriate value creation lever to pull can vary greatly from one company to another. Therefore, this book starts by giving an introduction to a framework for assessing and analyzing value creation and to better understand the balance and interplay between the three value drivers: **ROIC, growth,** and **cost of capital**.

We have seen that, in order to establish the correct starting point for the priorities, it is essential to examine the relationship between the ROIC and the cost of capital. From a valuation perspective, the benefit of focusing on profitability is very high when ROIC is close to the cost of capital.

Undoubtedly, growth plays an essential role in creating shareholder value. Nevertheless, as the value creation formula shows, growth is a double-edged sword, as growth only adds value if the company's profitability beats the cost of capital.

When it comes to the cost of capital, we show that by using the WACC construct, you may end up being "precisely wrong" rather than "roughly right". And when it comes to cost of capital, "roughly right" will do just fine! There are several "points of reference" in order to get it "roughly right". We prefer to use a DCF model to back-track the market's implied required return in combination with "earnings quality" approach (which is a subject we will get back to in Chapter 4).

References

Chancellor E (2015) Capital Returns: Investing Through the Capital Cycle: A Money Manager's Reports 2002–15. Palgrave Macmillan.

Chung KH, Wright P, Charoenwong C (1998) Investment Opportunities and Market Reaction to Capital Expenditure Decisions. Journal of Banking & Finance 22(1):41–60.

Damodaran (2023) Damodaran Online. https://pages.stern.nyu.edu/~adamodar/. Accessed 15 March 2023.

ECB (2018) Measuring and Interpreting the Cost of Equity in the Euro Area. Published online. https://www.ecb.europa.eu/pub/economic-bulletin/articles/2018/html/ecb.ebart201804_02.en.html.

Graham JR (2022) Presidential Address: Corporate Finance and Reality. Journal of Finance 77(4):1975–2049.

Magretta J (2012) Understanding Michael Porter—The Essential Guide to Competition and Strategy. Harvard Business Review Press.

McConnell JJ, Muscarella CJ (1985) Corporate Capital Expenditure Decisions and the Market Value of the Firm. Journal of Financial Economics 14(3):399–422.

McKinsey (2006) Balancing ROIC and Growth to Build Value. Published online. https://www.mckinsey.com/capabilities/strategy-and-corporate-finance/our-insights/balancing-roic-and-growth-to-build-value.

McKinsey & Company, Koller T, Goedhart M, Wessels D (2020). Valuation: Measuring and Managing the Value of Companies. Wiley.

Porter M E (1980) Competitive Strategy. Free Press.

PwC (2022) Riskpremien på den svenska aktiemarknaden. Published online. https://www.pwc.se/sv/corporate-finance/riskpremiestudien-2022.pdf.

Raynor ME, Ahmed M (2013) The Three Rules: How Exceptional Companies Think. Penguin Publishing Group.

CHAPTER 3

Market-Based Insights to Capital Allocation

Our ambition with this chapter is to supplement the analytical framework we just reviewed with empirical findings. We do that by taking a market-based approach in trying to shed some light on the delicate question of capital allocation and shareholder value creation. We use a Total Shareholder Return (TSR) framework to measure and better understand the drivers of a Nordic peer-group's value creation during a 14-year period ending in 2020.

Given the seemingly high volatility in the stock market, you might question the link between valuation theory and market prices. Since it is an important part of the allocation puzzle, we tested the link by applying the basic value formula presented in the previous chapter with inputs based on market expectations for profitability and growth. The discount rate was assessed based on margin volatility. Based on this simple methodology, we find a very strong correlation between expectations in the underlying performance drivers and the long-term stock market valuation. That is not the same thing as saying that the market's expectations of the fundamental drivers necessarily are correct at any point in time. However, we can expect that the stock market, at least over the longer term, will to a large degree reflect the fundamental or "intrinsic" value of a company, given the information available to the market. Or as the "father" of value

T. Arenbo, *Capital Allocation and Value Creation*,
https://doi.org/10.1007/978-3-031-47048-6_3

investing, Benjamin Graham, put it: "*In the short run, the market is a voting machine but in the long run, it is a weighing machine.*"

Furthermore, and just as importantly, it enables us to utilize the information conveyed in the marketplace to enhance the capital allocation decisions.

A Description of the Total Shareholder Return Framework

TSR is an important measure when evaluating the overall performance of a company's stock over a given period of time, taking into account both capital appreciation and the distribution of free cash flow to investors in the form of debt repayment, dividends, and share buybacks. By analyzing the different factors that influence TSR, investors as well as executives can gain a much better insights into a company's real value drivers.

To calculate the capital appreciation component of the TSR, three main factors are considered: sales growth, margin increase, and changes in the valuation multiple. Sales growth refers to the increase in revenue generated by the company over time, while margin increase reflects any improvements in the company's profitability. Changes in the valuation multiple capture changes in investors' long-term expectations regarding the company's future growth prospects, ROIC, and cost of capital.

Moreover, TSR is influenced by the way in which a company distributes its free cash flow to investors. A company may choose to allocate its free cash flow towards debt repayment, dividends, or share buybacks. Debt repayment can increase the company's creditworthiness and financial stability, while dividends and share buybacks can directly benefit shareholders by providing them with a share of the company's profits or by reducing the number of shares outstanding (Fig. 3.1).

There are several benefits of using the TSR model to evaluate a company's performance. For instance, the TSR model can be used to evaluate the effectiveness of a company's management team. By analyzing the TSR over multiple periods of time, investors can gain insights into whether management's decisions and capital allocation strategies are leading to improved shareholder returns or not.

The TRS model relates to the value drivers model presented in the previous chapter. However, the match between the models is not perfect as the variable of cost of capital is not directly observable in the marketplace. In the TSR model, changes in the cost of capital can constitute

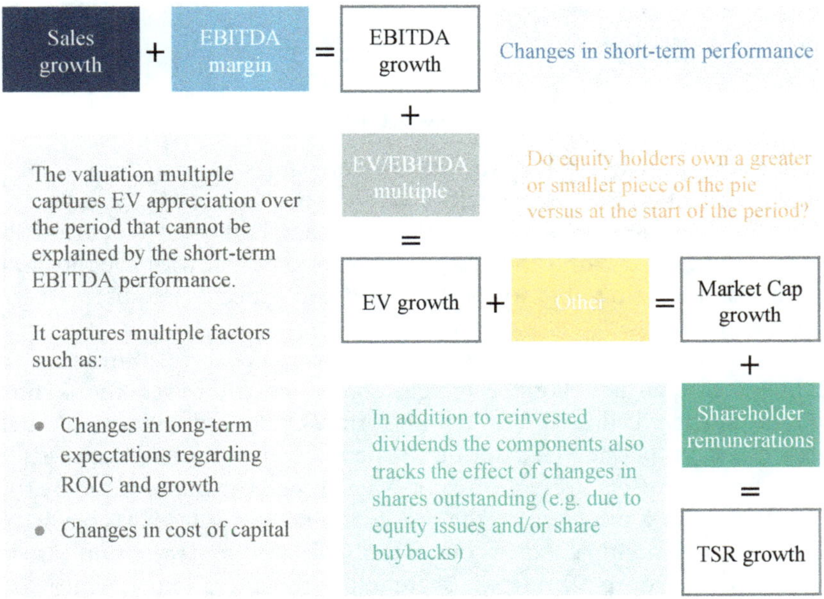

Fig. 3.1 TSR decomposition

an important part of the changes in the EV/EBITDA multiple. Furthermore, as the TSR model is forward-looking, no direct observations are available for ROIC either. The value-driving effects of ROIC primarily show up in the model as changes in the EBITDA margin and the EV/EBITDA multiple.

Peer-Group TSR Study

We now turn to our comprehensive TSR study and our findings around market-based value creation. Our study encompasses 148 Nordic companies that have been listed during the 2006–2020 period. We have excluded companies that had the majority of their operations within the following sectors: energy, utilities, real estate, or financials.

We have chosen to do our study over a fairly long time period for two reasons. Firstly, we prefer to have the entry and exit market values at roughly the same stages of the market cycle. Secondly, and more importantly, the TSR measurement is over shorter periods, strongly affected by market expectations.

General Findings—A Brief Summary

There are as many stories as there are companies behind the numbers presented in Fig. 3.2. Nonetheless, several conclusions can be drawn at the aggregated level. On average, the total sample median is remarkably close to where we expect the cost of capital to be (8%), with roughly 50% of the sample being able to meet or beat the expected required return over the period.

As can be seen, in isolation, growth has been a positive contributor to TSR for all quartiles. For the margin component, however, the picture is more scattered. Basically, all top performers managed to increase or at least maintain their margins during the period, which was not the case for the other groups. As a result, investors valued the growth produced by the first quartile at a premium to the rest of the sample. This is visible as an EV/EBITDA multiple expansion in Fig. 3.2. The fourth strong return driver for the top performers is shareholder remuneration activities, i.e. dividends and share buybacks. In our methodology, however, it should be noted that the dividends are reinvested in the share, and returns from this TSR driver are thus reinforced by a rising share price.

Having reviewed the cornerstones in valuation theory in the previous chapter, we would expect ROIC and growth to be the main drivers of TSR over longer time periods. However, as can be seen in Fig. 3.2, the best quartile had a very large performance contribution from multiple expansion. Why was this a driving factor only for the top quartile? To answer that question, we need to better understand how the market is valuing the fundamental drivers, and we start by looking at ROIC.

ROIC—Where It All Starts

Before describing the ROIC characteristics of the various quartiles, it is worth refreshing a few things from the previous chapter. First, not all companies are suitable for being measured by ROIC. ROIC is typically exaggerated for companies with a thin asset base, as well as for companies

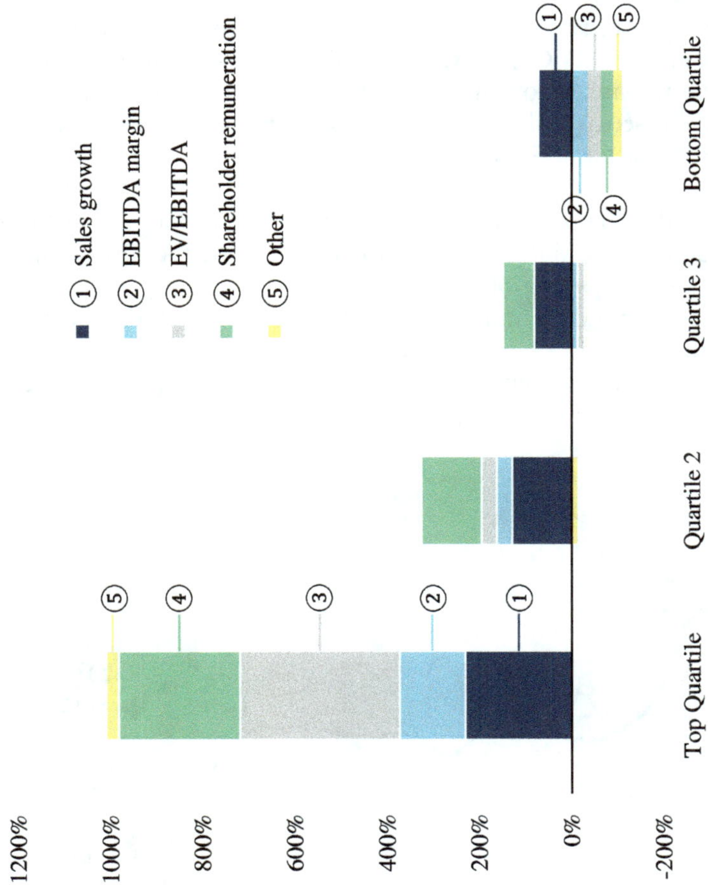

Fig. 3.2 TSR decomposition per quartile

with a very high share of expensed R&D. Furthermore, it is important to measure ROIC both with and without goodwill, as this indicates two very different things. ROIC without goodwill gives us a good indication of how good the company is at creating value organically, whereas ROIC including goodwill also gives an indication of the M&A skills of the company.

In the previous chapter, we claimed that characteristics driving the level and persistency of ROIC, for example in the form of competitive advantage, are tightly linked to valuation. Turning to our sample, we can see that our claim seems to hold as a clear ROIC pattern emerges between the different quartiles (Fig. 3.3).

- 95% of the companies in the top quartile have had a median ROIC (including goodwill) over the period that is above the cost of capital, with a group average of 18.5%
- The corresponding number for quartile 2 is 79% of companies beating their cost of capital, with an average ROIC of 11.7%
- Quartile 3 displays similar numbers, with 72% beating cost of capital and an average ROIC of 10.1%

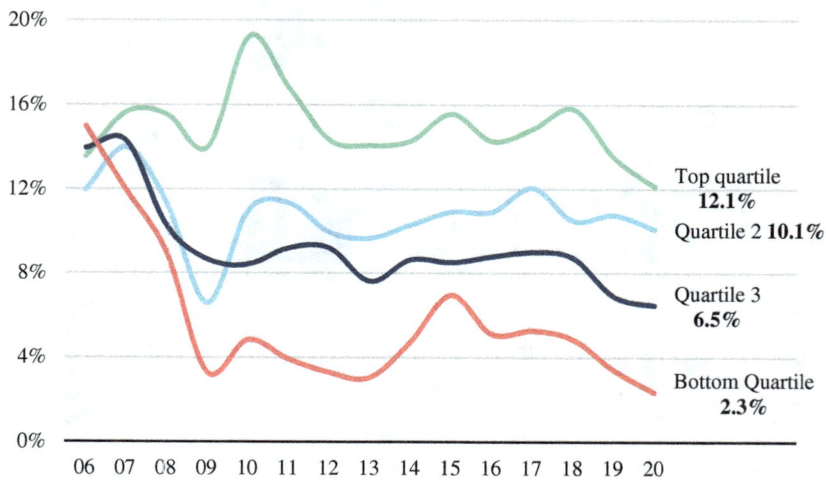

Fig. 3.3 Median ROIC development per quartile (Dec 2006–Dec 2020)

- For the bottom quartile, only 29% produced a positive return spread and the ROIC average only reached 5.7%.

The results strongly confirm the findings from the previous chapter about ROIC being at the centre of fundamental value creation. Over a time period of almost 15 years, we would normally expect ROIC to display mean-reversion characteristics. After all, economic theory tells us that ROIC in excess of the cost of capital should be erased by competition. However, our sample data does not show any such tendencies over the measurement period.

Growth—A Double-Edged Sword

When analyzing growth we wanted to find out how large a part of the quartiles could be defined as "**fast growing**".[1] It turned out that 70% of the top quartile companies had sales growth that, according to our definition, qualified to be categorized as fast growing. The corresponding numbers for the other three quartiles were considerably lower (quartile 2 = 30%, quartile 3 = 20%, and quartile 4 = 13%).

However, as we saw in the previous section, growth alone does not do the trick. It has to be accompanied by a return that is higher than the cost of capital in order to be value creating. In our top quartile, all of the 26 companies that qualified for the fast-growing group managed to grow with a ROIC above the cost of capital. For the other quartiles, the corresponding numbers were 8 out of 11 for quartile 2, 5 out of 7 for quartile 3, and 0 out of 5 for quartile 4.

We can connect the ROIC and growth discussion with **cash flow deployment**, i.e. how much of the total cash flow is consumed by growth initiatives. Thanks to the high ROIC levels, it turns out that a median top performer only had to spend around 20% of cash flow from operations (CFO) on organic growth.[2] That is considerably less than the rest of the sample. On the other hand, it spent some 30% on acquisitions, which is well above the peer-group average. For the total peer group, somewhat above of 50% of CFO was allocated towards organic and acquired growth.

[1] We defined a company as fast growing if its sales grew at least twice as fast as nominal GDP over the period.

[2] The necessary investment rate to achieve a given growth rate will be lower for a high ROIC company (Investment rate = Growth/ROIC).

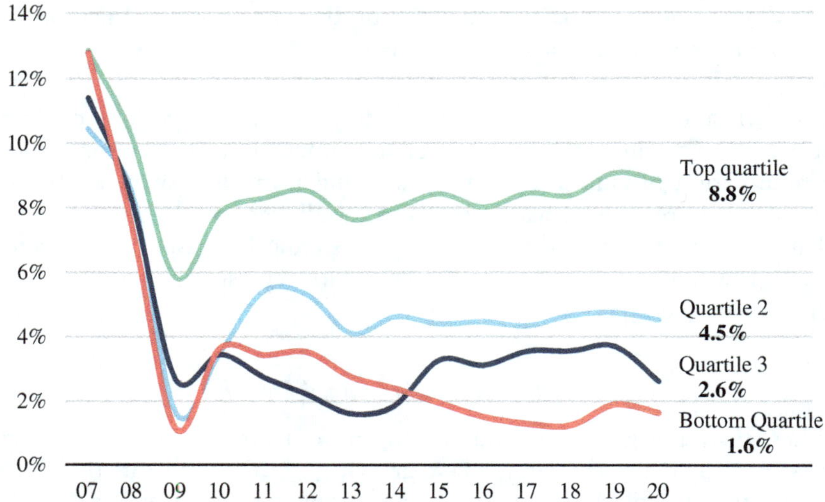

Fig. 3.4 Median growth development per quartile (2007–2020)

Quartiles 1–3 all showed similar overall levels, but quartile 4 lagged due to lower spending on acquisitions (Fig. 3.4).

Margin Stability and the Cost of Capital

As we touched upon in the introduction, value-creating growth and improved margins/ROIC are not the only ways a company can create value. The third value-driving factor, cost of capital, can play a very important role as well. Out of the three fundamental value drivers, however, cost of capital is more elusive and depends on factors like earnings quality, market sentiment, confidence in management, and capital structure. As a very simple proxy for cost of capital, we have constructed a measure we call the margin volatility ratio. The margin volatility does not seem to play any significant part in the valuation of companies with the highest growth. However, for the majority of companies, margin volatility seems to matter much more. Thus, factors like pricing power and a flexible cost structure not only affect value through higher profitability but also through a lower cost of capital. This is a topic we will return to in Chapter 4.

When it comes to our sample, quartile 1 has the highest "margin quality", followed by quartile 2 and quartile 3. Quartile 4 is lagging quite

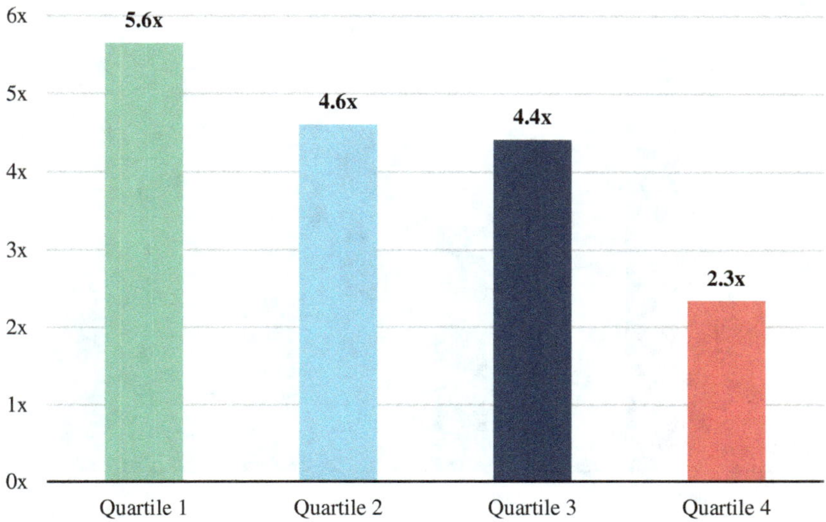

Fig. 3.5 Average "margin quality" per quartile (Dec 2006–Dec 2020)

considerably, and it seems reasonable to assume that there is a clear effect on the cost of capital between the quartiles (Fig. 3.5).

Valuation Multiples per Quartiles

We can now summarize the fundamental value drivers by comparing market-based and theoretical multiples. As can be seen in Fig. 3.6, the average EV/EBITDA multiple for the top and bottom quartiles are around 16× and 6×, respectively. This turns out to be very close to what can be justified by our simple long-term market-based valuation model. In terms of expected fundamental value drivers for the top quartile, our model assumes an average ROIC of 15%, a growth rate of 3.6%, and a cost of capital of 6.6%.The corresponding fourth quartile numbers are ROIC = 9%, growth = 1.7% and cost of capital = 8.6%

The multiple expansion (see Fig. 3.2) can thus be explained by changes in the market expectations of the three underlying value drivers between 2006 and 2020. And again, we see a strong correlation between theory and long-term market pricing.

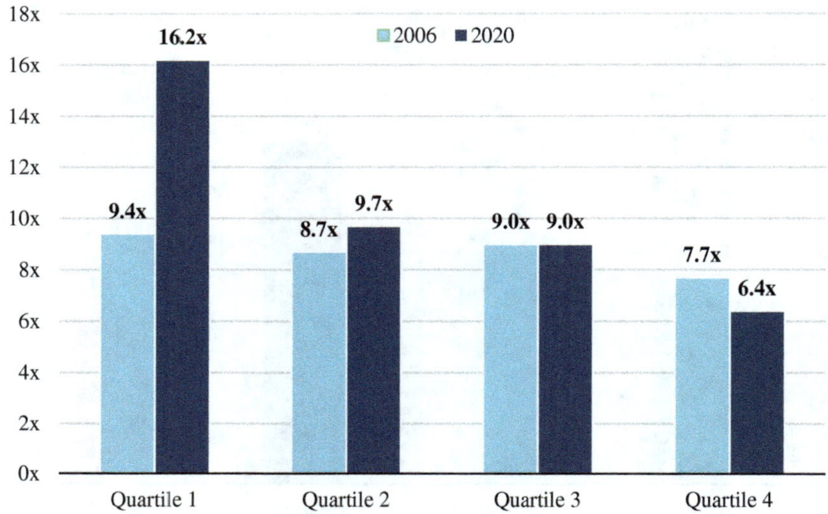

Fig. 3.6 12m forward-looking EV/EBITDA multiple per quartile

Top and Bottom Performers—A Head-to-Head Comparison

We now turn to a more qualitative review of the sample, where we look for common denominators in the best and worst performing quartiles respectively.

Top Performers

When we try to sort the top performers by their drivers of outperformance, it is not surprising that high growth turns out to be a key feature. And remember that they all grew with a return above the required cost of capital!

We can sort the companies into four rough categories (where some companies can be found in several buckets). We have a group with very **strong organic growth**, often coupled with a high ROIC (making the growth "cheap"). Here we find companies like NIBE, Nordic Semiconductor, Tomra, Hexagon, Novo Nordisk, Coloplast, Kongsberg Gruppen, and GN Store Nord.

The largest group consists of companies with a very **high acquisition activity** (in some cases, coupled with high organic growth). In this category, we find three groups of companies; service companies

(Sweco, ÅF, Knowit, Etteplan), industrial consolidators (BeijerRef, NIBE, Addnode, DSV, Proact, Per Aarsleff), and investment companies (Indutrade, Addtech, OEM). This group is dominated by serial acquirers that often target privately owned companies. These are the companies that display the highest multiple expansion reflecting expectations of a high future acquisition activity as well as a high profitability on the acquisitions.

Another set of companies has a very **high and stable ROIC**. Many companies in this sector turn out to be market leader within their respective industries. These are companies with high pricing power and stable margins, which enables them to have both a high pay-out ratio and a low discount rate. In this group, we find names like Novo Nordisk, Simcorp, Atlas Copco, Swedish Match, Coloplast, KONE, and Elisa. The multiple contribution factor for these companies is positive but much less pronounced than for the fast-growing group.

The last group of companies managed to achieve either a **business transformation or a strong margin improvement**. The Danish brewing company Royal Unibrew managed to transform itself from a supply-focused commodity producer to a consumer-oriented niche producer of beverages. Nolato, on the other hand, managed to transform itself from a regional component supplier into a global partner that supplies end-to-end solutions. Common to all successful turnarounds is that they started by strengthening the balance sheet by share issues and/or divestments in combination with cost-cutting programmes. As a second leg in the turn-around journey, they launched a new strategy focused on profitable organic growth. Some of the cases involved a very active portfolio management with large divestments and subsequent acquisitions. In Chapters 5 and 6, we will look further into this topic.

In summary, there are various paths that can result in a high-performing position. The majority of the companies in our selection reached the top thanks to a combination of strong organic growth and/or growth through acquisitions, along with a high ROIC. On the other hand, if growth prospects are low, a high profitability and high cash distribution to shareholders can also be a winning strategy. The third significant group of high-performing companies consists of those that managed to turn their struggling business around. Their primary driver of TSR is an improvement in margins and subsequently ROIC (Fig. 3.7).

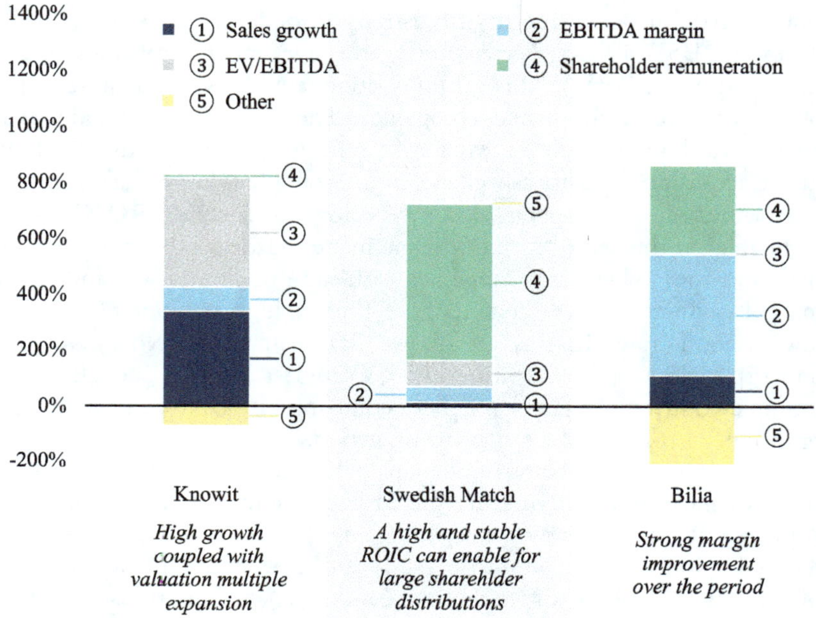

Fig. 3.7 Multiple roads lead to Rome—Quartile 1 companies with similar TSR performance but different drivers (Dec 2006–Dec 2020)

Bottom Performers

If there is one common denominator among the laggards, it is, not surprisingly, that a majority of the companies struggled to reach sufficiently high ROIC levels. The most common explanation for having a low profitability stems from being in a sector that experienced **overinvestments** during the period. Among these sectors, we find steel producers, airline carriers, telecom equipment manufacturers, transportation companies, and meat processors.

The supply-side discipline in the sectors above will to a large extent determine whether these companies can restore their profitability, which in turn will be a very important factor for what quartile they will end up in over the coming period.

Acquisitions turn out to be a relatively large group for the bottom performers as well. Maybe it does not come as a surprise that we see a different kind of M&As in this category compared to the top performers.

Companies like Telia, Sanoma, and Elanders made acquisitions in order to boost growth outside their slow-growing domestic market. Some other companies did large public deals, as when the Swedish steel company SSAB bought the Canadian peer company IPSCO right before the global financial crisis.

Large acquisitions outside your home markets seem to be a recipe for low returns. ITAB, Lindab, Husqvarna, and, as mentioned, SSAB are examples of companies in the quartile that all made acquisitions that led to a materially higher operational as well as financial risk.

Another group of companies struggled with **low or negative organic growth** and relatively low margins. Profitability takes a hit when demand falls and scale advantages become diluted. The companies' asset base often takes longer to depreciate compared to the rate of change in demand, and too much capital get stuck in the sector for too long.

For yet another group of companies, the market attached **too-high-earnings expectations** going into our measurement period. These companies struggled to live up to high growth expectations and elevated multiples, and thus in many cases experienced a multiple contraction. Here we find companies with fairly well-performing ROIC like Uponor, Oriola, Clas Ohlson, Nobia, and FLSmidth.

Another category in the bottom quartile consists of companies exposed to the **commodity cycle**. The companies in this group had among the worst ROIC volatility ratios[3] in the sample. A volatile and low profitability is an indication of low pricing power—not a favoured feature among investors.

High indebtedness added to the woes for the bottom performers, and around 50% became financially distressed[4] during the global financial crisis, out of which more than half had leverage that was too high when entering the crises. In Chapter 8, we will look into the subject of capital structure in more detail.

[3] ROIC volatility ratio is calculated by dividing the ROIC average by the standard deviation.

[4] Defined as Debt/Enterprise Value above 50%.

Is There a Destiny with Belonging to a Sector?

From the analysis of the bottom performers, you might get the impression that belonging to a sector comes with a destiny that is hard to escape. But being in a sector does not have to mean there is a destiny. For instance, out of our four telecom companies, Elisa qualifies as a top performer, Tele2 makes it to the second quartile, while Telia and Telenor end up in the third quartile. In another large Nordic sector—the pulp and paper industry—the same pattern is visible where Holmen, Billerud-Korsnäs, UPM-Kymmene, Mätsa Board, Stora Enso, and Rottneros are spread out over three different quartiles. When we look at the seven companies in our peer group belonging to the consultancy industry, the picture is more homogeneous, where all but one make it to the top-40 list. The laggard, Tieto, failed to grow in line with peers partly due to a deviating acquisition strategy.

Thus, capital allocation can really make a difference. In the next section, we will try to dig further into and analyze this skill by conducting two case studies: Royal Unibrew and Carlsberg, on the one hand, and Telia and Elisa, on the other (Fig. 3.8).

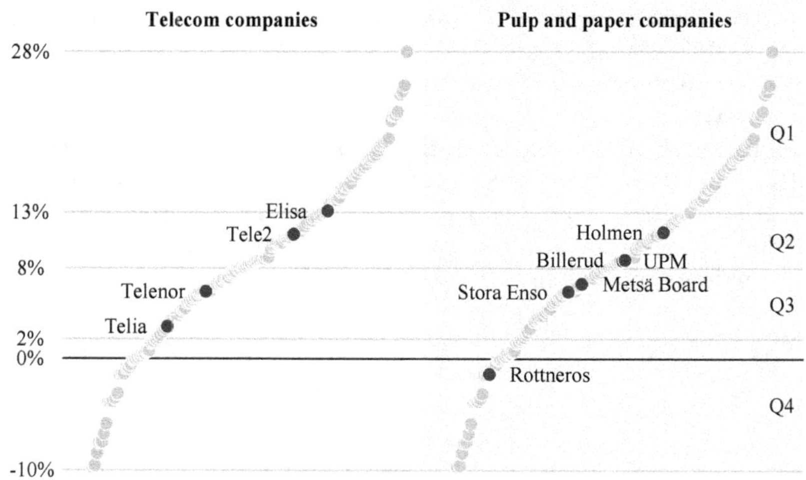

Fig. 3.8 TSR CAGR distribution for the telecom and pulp and paper companies

Case Study: Royal Unibrew vs Carlsberg

The small Danish brewing company Royal Unibrew managed to make it to the top performing quartile despite having a tough start and being active in relatively mature markets. Coming into the period, it shared a failed M&A-driven growth strategy with its bigger Danish cousin Carlsberg. However, the divergence in shareholder return between the two companies in the second part of the period is remarkable and deserves a closer look (Fig. 3.9).

The Pre-crisis Period (2006–2009)—Focus on Growth

Coming into the period, the commoditized brewing industry was in a rapid consolidation phase with a focus on market-leading positions that could unlock production and distribution scale advantages. This was well illustrated in 2005 when Royal Unibrew set a growth target of 50% for the coming three years.

As a consequence, Royal Unibrew and Carlsberg both pursued ambitious international growth strategies. With large debt-funded acquisitions

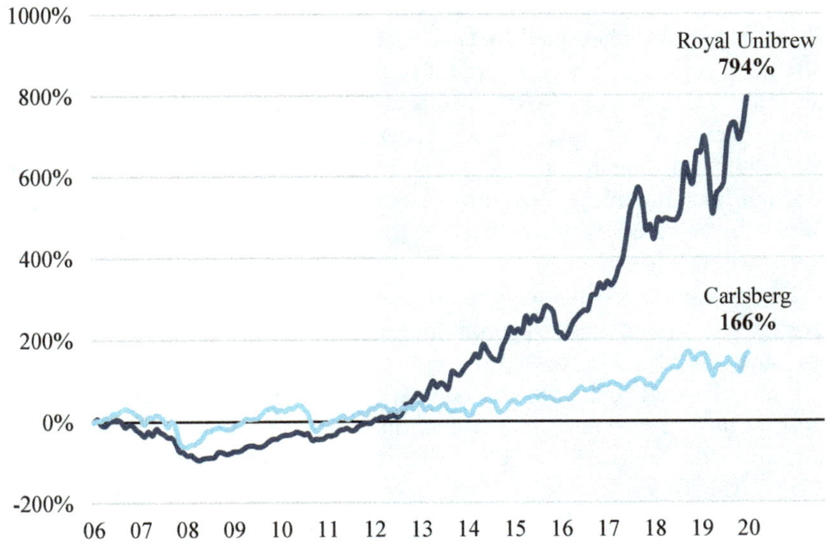

Fig. 3.9 TSR development (Dec 2006–Dec 2020)

of breweries in Poland and the Caribbean for the former and in Russia for the latter, the turmoil in connection with the global financial crisis came to test the value accretion of those deals. Simultaneously, the sector dynamics were about to change with decreasing production costs and new consumer preferences following the introduction of new premium products.

For Royal Unibrew, these shifts were a rude awakening. Burdened by plummeting profits and an elevated leverage, the TSR was down 95% between the end of 2006 and the beginning of 2009. While this forced a complete change in the strategic agenda, the crisis also triggered an impressive post-crisis turnaround. For Carlsberg, however, the crisis was merely the beginning of a challenging period and what would serve as an example of the inherent risks associated with large acquisitions in new geographical markets.

The Post-crisis Period (2009–2012)

A net debt/enterprise value above 90% at the beginning of 2009 brought about a deleverage and profitability focus for Royal Unibrew, led by newly appointed CEO Henrik Brandt. In terms of financial targets, the strategy aimed at restoring net debt/EBITDA to below 2.5× and reaching an EBIT margin of 10% (hiked to 13% in 2010). This focus is apparent when looking at the cash flow deployment priorities and ROIC development for the 2009–2012 period. Royal Unibrew initiated a large portfolio restructuring (being a net seller over the period) where it divested both the Polish and Caribbean assets acquired as late as 2005–2007 to focus on core markets and niche positions. Together with an equity issue during 2009, the released funds enabled significant cash flows to be allocated towards debt reduction.

The new management team launched a successful four-year turnaround programme that included profitability-improving investments in production and distribution, overhead cost reductions, product mix changes, and an enhanced focus on various marketing initiatives. These initiatives resulted in an impressive increase in margins and ROIC, with the latter climbing from below 5 to 20%. With healthy margins and leverage (net debt/EBITDA of around 0.5× at year-end 2012), the company was in good shape to handle the structural shifts in the industry, and thus ready for the next stage of the turnaround.

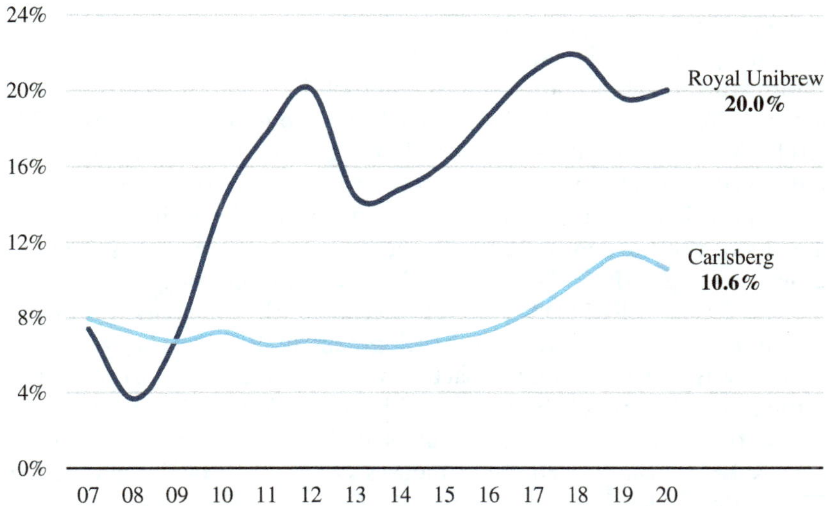

Fig. 3.10 ROIC including goodwill (2007–2020)

For Carlsberg, its overdependence on the Russian market would prove ill-fated. When the Russian government (in a fight against growing alcoholism) raised taxes and imposed advertising bans, this amplified the negative earnings effect from the financial crisis. Carlsberg did focus on operational efficiency and debt deleveraging but also remained committed to its strategy of building the "fastest growing global beer company". However, the company did not have the same positive development as Royal Unibrew when it came to EBITDA and ROIC, where the latter remained stable at around 6–7% (including goodwill) (Fig. 3.10).

From 2013 Onwards

In 2013, once profitability was restored, Royal Unibrew announced the acquisition of Hartwall. In terms of EV, Hartwall—the second-largest beverage producer in Finland—was around 60% the size of Royal Unibrew. In contrast to the Polish acquisition, Hartwall had well-invested assets and a product mix that complimented Royal Unibrew's, thereby leading to a reduced exposure to beer. This time, the synergies from the acquisition were there and the deal triggered an acceleration in both profits and shareholder returns. During 2013–2020, the company managed to grow organically (4% on average per year), and while the acquisition initially diluted the 20% ROIC, it soon started to climb back towards the pre-acquisition level. As a sign of the markets regaining confidence in Royal Unibrew's ability to achieve profitable growth, the EV/EBITDA multiple doubled to above 18x. At the same time, thanks to the high ROIC, Royal Unibrew spent more than 60% of the operating cash flow on dividends and share buybacks, further amplifying the TSR. When taking stock of the end of 2020, we see that the turnaround resulted in a rather amazing TSR of 794% since 2006—despite the tough start.

For Carlsberg, EBITDA started to decline as the company was unable to compensate for the negative development in Russia. The large debt position was also a constraining factor, with net debt/EBITDA remaining in the 2.5–3.0× range (the target had been <3×) since 2009. In the Q4 report for 2014, the company finally stated that its main areas of focus were ROIC and improved credit metrics. The launch of the new "SAIL '22" strategy (developed under new CEO Cees 't Hart) further underlined that inorganic growth would have a low priority going forward. Instead, initiatives and capital would be allocated with the ambition to raise organic growth and ROIC. By 2020, it was clear that the strategy had delivered the desired effect. Between 2015 and 2019, Carlsberg had average organic growth of around 3% and managed to raise ROIC to above 10% (including goodwill). This was well received by investors, and annual TSR was a strong 14.9% from the launch of the new strategy until the end of 2020.

Case Study Summary

This case study highlights a few important points about capital allocation:

- Trying to outgrow a mature market with acquisitions can come at a high cost
- Structural shifts that require a change in strategy also can occur in seemingly stable markets
- It is hard to turn a business around if you simultaneously carry a heavy debt burden
- Thus, improving profitability often goes hand in hand with balance sheet strengthening activities like divestments and/or share issuance
- That, in turn, requires management to be unsentimental about prior strategic mistakes and owners to commit to the new strategic route

- Once market confidence in the company and its management team is restored, the door to organic and acquired growth opens up again

Case Study: Elisa vs Telia

The telecom industry's entry barriers are high, with operators needing to win or buy frequency and then build a network. This leaves room for only a few operators. But even for the incumbents, it is all about scale, and market share gains are expensive. Market leader status gives potential efficiency gains with scale, which should result in higher margins than for challengers. That is what the textbook says, but what if the market leader is not robust enough to drive this efficiency and take advantage of its position? (Fig. 3.11).

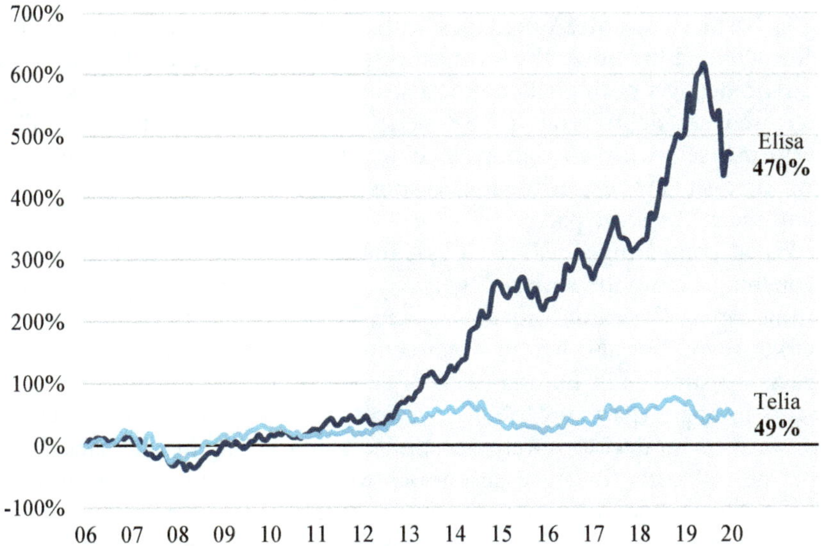

Fig. 3.11 TSR development (Dec 2006–Dec 2020)

The Local Challenger Versus an Expanding Market Leader

This is the story of the Nordic giant Telia, which holds the market-leading position in its core markets of Sweden, Finland, and the Baltic countries, versus Elisa, with its no. 2 mobile operator position in Finland and Estonia back in 2006. However, the annual TSR for Telia for 2006–2020 has amounted to a meagre 2.9%, while Elisa has yielded a stunning 13.2%. Why was the return so low for the market leader, and how could Elisa's outperformance have been so substantial? And if we instead take a starting point of 2013—when Elisa's outperformance began—the difference is even starker.

The First Period (2006–2013)—The Devil Is in the Details

Cash flow from operations grew slowly for both operators in this period, and their cash flow deployments towards growth were almost identical. Telia balanced its M&A activities with divestments, netting out at 0%. Meanwhile, Elisa took the next step, prioritizing higher allocation to shareholders via both dividends and share buybacks, financing these with increased net debt. From a TSR perspective, they showed very similar performances, with no sign from either that overall cash flow generation or cash flow deployment decisions suggesting that this would not continue at the same pace.

When comparing Telia and Elisa, though, we can see that a lot was happening below the surface, especially regarding where they were allocating capex. Capex decisions are a key factor for operators, influencing market share, but also margins indirectly. Telia invested for growth, with heavy investments in Eurasia (29% of capex) as well as greenfield investments in Spain (part of Mobility Services, at 31% of total capex). These two investment decisions were questioned by the equity market back then, but the full costs for these allocations were not settled until long after 2013. Meanwhile, Elisa invested in its core markets for strengthening market position and efficiency. And this paid off, with Elisa taking over as the market share leader from Telia within mobile.

The Second Period (2014–2020)—Time to Harvest the Investments

Telia had invested heavily ahead of this period, but instead of growing, its cash flow had decreased by 2020 versus 2013. In addition, it needed to allocate a greater proportion of cash flow into capex. Its new "back to core markets" strategy can also be seen in the large divestments that brought losses rather than the hoped-for gains—not a good harvest. Moreover, it then made expensive acquisitions in its home markets (TV4 and Get, among others) in an attempt to gain synergies and secure growth opportunities. Given the unchanged net debt, but lower allocation to shareholders, the equity story for this dividend-driven share took a beating.

The pay-off from Elisa's investments was already starting to be seen in 2014, when cash flow started to grow, as the integration project unlocked improved efficiency (higher EBITDA margins) and market share gains. Thanks to its strengthened market position and improved profitability, Elisa could start investing for growth, adding new services, and entering new markets without increasing capex allocations. In a sector where dividends are key to the equity story, Elisa had managed to add a growth angle that was superior to that of its sector peers.

The Evidence

Split into these two periods, Elisa is the shining star, with superior organic and acquired growth, while Telia's investments have yielded poorly.

While Telia's ROIC fell in 2014 and has continued to slowly slide from that point, Elisa's well placed investments can be seen in its increasing ROIC, regardless of whether we include goodwill or not (Fig. 3.12).

Case Study Summary

This case study highlights a few important points about capital allocation:

- The long-term strategy around investment decisions will have a substantial impact on TSR in a capex-intense industry
- Looking for growth outside home markets is a more risky strategy, for which a company can pay a very high price, as Telia's performance demonstrates. Meanwhile, Elisa has been able to invest in

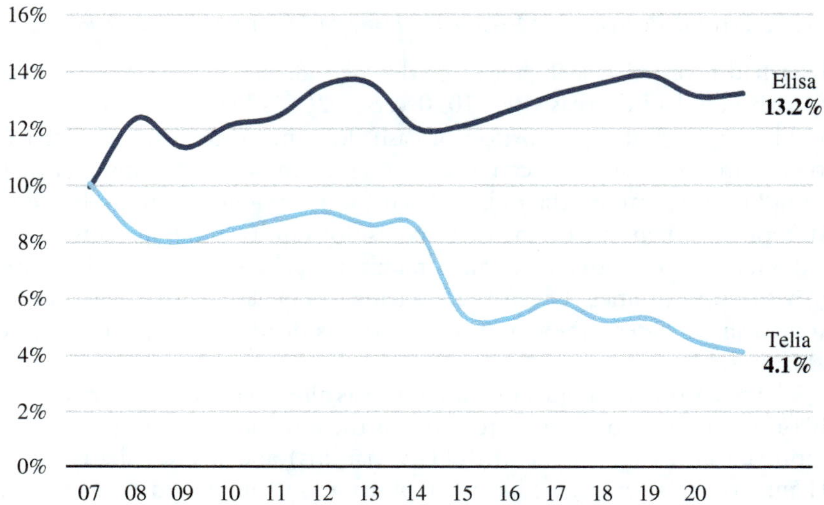

Fig. 3.12 ROIC including goodwill (2007–2020)

"quality" in its home market and has strengthened its position versus competitors

- In addition, it takes time for the effect from small under-investments to hit EBITDA and impact the crux of the equity story: dividends.

Conclusions

In this chapter, we have aimed to find market-based insights on how to improve corporate executives' capital allocation skills. Not surprisingly, there is no single formula for a successful capital allocation strategy. However, a good starting point is to understand the historical drivers of TSR, as well as being able to read the market expectations conveyed in the relevant valuation multiples.

Among other things, we conclude that:

- Our studies clearly show that a large part of the companies ending up in the bottom quartile have done so due to poor capital allocation decisions. Many poor decisions could probably have been avoided if corporate managers would have had a more profound knowledge and understanding of the theory of corporate value creation. But we also believe that many mistakes could have been avoided if managers would have had a better knowledge and understanding of the financial markets.

- Since the GFC growth has been in vogue among investors, but it is a double-edged sword. This may be somewhat surprising, but it turns out that high growth only is a very strong driver of value creation for a relatively limited number of companies.
- For a large proportion of the companies, increased profitability and margin stability would bring much greater reward in terms of shareholder value than aiming for higher growth. This is a topic we will look further into in the next chapter.
- The winners in the "high profitability" group seem not only to be proficient in running their operations efficiently, but also in knowing what to do and not to do from a strategic perspective. By mastering the typical investor skill of portfolio allocation, they increased the odds of becoming a top performer. In Chapters 5 and 6, we will take a deep dive into the topic of portfolio strategy when we look into M&A and review the case of creating value with divestments and spin-offs.

Reference

BCG (2015) Value Creation for the Rest of Us—The 2015 Value Creators Report. Published online. https://web-assets.bcg.com/img-src/BCG-Value-Creation-for-the-Rest-of-Us-Jul-2015_tcm9-171215.pdf.

CHAPTER 4

Earnings quality

We end part one of this book with a chapter where we discuss the, sometimes overlooked, importance of earnings quality as a value driver. In particular, we focus on the way earnings quality and cost of capital can be linked together.

Even though growth has been in vogue among investors for some time now, value can, as we saw in the last chapter, be created in other ways as well. One investor that especially stands out when it comes to earnings quality as a driver of performance is Berkshire Hathaway. They have a long history of investing in companies with strong competitive advantages and durable business models. Buffett has often referred to this as investing in companies with an "economic moat", which helps protect their profitability and market share over the long term.

Buffett has been known to avoid companies that prioritize growth at the expense of earnings quality or margin resilience. Instead, he looks for companies with a strong track record of profitability, stable and predictable earnings, and a history of generating high levels of cash flow.

There is little doubt that risk plays an important role in valuation, but how could management think about the link between earnings quality and shareholder value creation?

T. Arenbo, *Capital Allocation and Value Creation*,
https://doi.org/10.1007/978-3-031-47048-6_4

What is Earnings Quality?

In academic studies, "earnings quality" is typically defined as the extent to which a company's reported earnings accurately reflect its underlying economic performance. This is often measured using various financial metrics that can capture different aspects of earnings manipulation or information asymmetry. However, our focus is on the way investors perceive earnings quality and its relationship to valuation. Common measures of earnings quality include:

- Predictability: This refers to the extent to which a company's future earnings can be forecasted based on its past performance.
- Persistence: This refers to the likelihood of a company's current earnings to continue into future periods.
- Accruals and reporting quality: This measures the degree to which a company's reported earnings rely on accrual accounting estimates, which are more susceptible to manipulation compared to cash-based earnings.
- Conservatism: This measures the tendency of a company's accounting policies to understate rather than overstate its earnings.
- Timeliness: This refers to the promptness and accuracy with which a company reports its earnings.

The choice of measure for earnings quality depends on the purpose and the availability of data. As mentioned, different measures capture different aspects of earnings quality and may have different implications for shareholder returns.

Quantifying Earnings Quality

Measuring the quality of earnings is a complex task, often complicated by the absence of a clear definition and insufficient data required for measurement. If the focus, for instance, is on the reporting aspect of earnings quality, one should try to understand the dynamics between the income and cash flow statements. If a company's accruals are increasing faster than its cash flows, it may imply aggressive accounting practices that could distort its reported earnings. Additionally, it may be worth investigating the amount of non-operating items, such as asset sales, as these types of earnings are often less reliable.

However, when it comes to investors, the top two items on the list above—predictability and persistency—tend to be the main focus. This is also how we prefer to evaluate earnings quality. To provide a simple measure of this aspect of earnings quality, we have developed what we call the "margin volatility ratio". This basic measure is calculated by dividing the standard deviation of the operating margin by the average margin. See Fig. 4.1.

This approach is very similar to the way in which the rating agency Standard & Poor's complements its qualitative assessment of a company's business risk profile with quantitative measures. Specifically, they use the EBITDA margin standard error of regression for a period of at least seven years and compare it to the average EBITDA margin for a mixed historical and forward-looking five-year period.

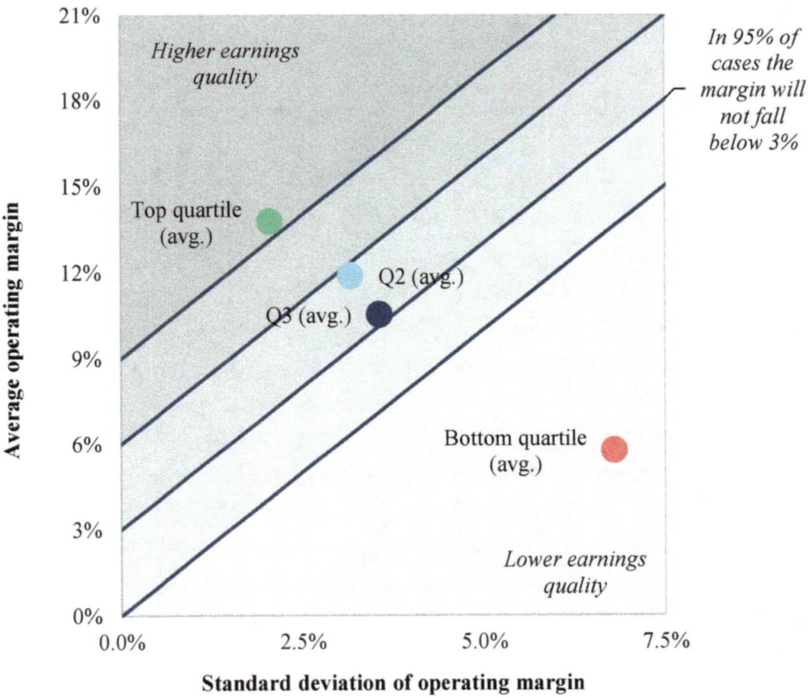

Fig. 4.1 "Margin volatility ratio"

A clear connection between a rating agency's business risk assessment and the (unlevered) cost of equity of a company becomes evident. This is because the cash flow that pays both debt holders and equity holders is the same. This connection was elegantly established by Robert C. Merton (1974).[1]

Margin Volatility and Valuation

When we tested our proxy for earnings quality on our Nordic sample group, we discovered that margin volatility displayed a higher overall correlation with excess return than ROIC and growth did. The graph below illustrates the relationship between the margin volatility ratio and the EBIT/EV multiple. As demonstrated, there is a clear correlation between our proxy measure for earnings quality and valuation for low-growth companies. However, for high growth companies, the margin volatility ratio appears to be of much less significance. See Fig. 4.2.

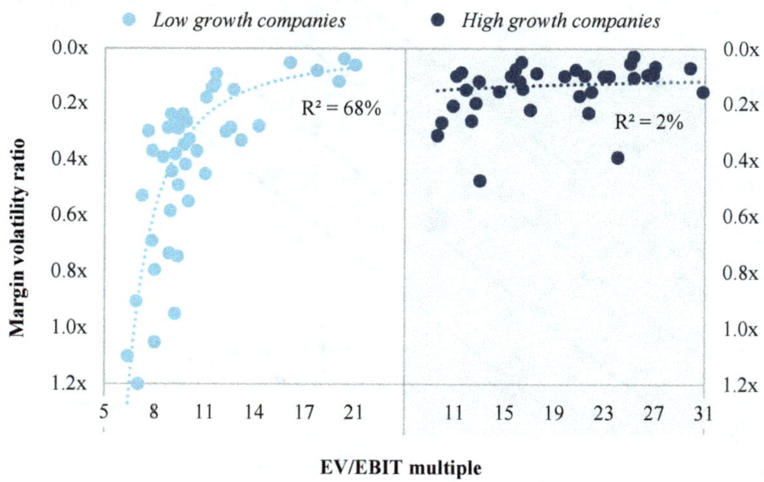

Fig. 4.2 The correlation between our proxy measure for earnings quality and valuation differs between high and low-growth companies

[1] The Merton model stipulates that the credit risk of a company can be assessed by modelling the value of a put option on the assets owned by the company.

Evaluating the quality of earnings is often subjective, and different investors may have varying opinions on what constitutes high-quality earnings. Moreover, the challenge of finding a suitable quantitative method to measure earnings quality adds further uncertainty to its impact on shareholder value creation. Despite the challenges in establishing a robust theoretical platform for analyzing earnings quality and its impact on valuation, there is no doubt about the critical role that earnings quality has to play in any CEO's capital allocation framework.

Business Strategy

It has been surprisingly difficult to find research on the link between the kinds of earnings quality that we are interested in, namely, the persistency and predictability of earnings, and the cost of capital. Academic research seems to focus more on the area of accrued and reported quality of earnings. However, we will attempt to shed some light on the subject and hope that our case study review presented below may serve as inspiration for managers seeking ideas and strategies for improving earnings quality.

Again, we examined our Nordic peer group, this time choosing to take a closer look at the top quarter that had shown the greatest improvement in their margin stability ratio during the surveyed period. Although analyzing business strategies is somewhat beyond the scope of this book, it is difficult to completely avoid the subject in a book aimed at enhancing shareholder value creation. While scrutinizing the underlying factors behind the enhanced margin stability, business strategy takes a central position in one way or another. After evaluating our peer group, we choose to summarize the primary strategies used to enhance margin stability into the following four categories:

1. Operational excellence

At the top of the list for achieving operational excellence and high-quality earnings is often an increased focus on the **core business**. This typically involves a company allocating its resources and efforts towards the products and services that it excels in and where it has the strongest competitive advantage. We can find several examples of companies which during our reviewed period have had an increased focus on the core business, including Orkla, Stora Enso, UPM, and Nokia, to name a few.

A second factor of importance in achieving higher margin stability has been the implementation of a **flexible cost base**. It is crucial for companies to be able to adjust their costs quickly in response to, for example, lower demand. Outsourcing certain functions and processes, as well as employing part of the workforce on flexible terms, are common examples of methods used for increasing cost flexibility. This has been a popular strategy for a long time, and among the companies on our list pursuing this strategy, we find, for example, Atlas Copco, Electrolux, Kone, Sandvik, and Volvo.

In addition, several companies have mentioned implementing improved performance management systems that align employee performance with the company's strategic goals. They are also investing in IT systems to enhance logistics and supply chain management. Additionally, the majority of companies regularly implement cost-cutting measures to reduce operating expenses. In some cases, risk management frameworks are also mentioned as a means of improving operational excellence.

2. Low cyclicality

One approach that the companies commonly used to mitigate the negative effects of sales cyclicality was to try to expand the share of **aftermarket sales** and build **strong customer relationships**. When a company prioritizes aftermarket sales, it can generate a reliable and consistent revenue stream that is less susceptible to the cyclical nature of new sales. Furthermore, by offering high-quality aftermarket products and services, a company can create loyalty and trust among its customers. Several companies in our peer group, such as Konecranes, Hexagon, and Atlas Copco, have successfully employed this strategy.

3. Pricing power

Having a strong pricing power is a highly effective means of achieving greater margin stability, especially in times of volatile inflation. One strategy frequently employed by the companies surveyed was to increase their pricing power by focusing on **niche markets**. By targeting niche markets, where there may be less competition and a higher degree of customer loyalty, companies can gain market leadership positions and greater control over pricing. This approach has also been commonly adopted by our peers, and we can see several companies on the list that have successfully implemented this strategy, such as Atlas Copco, Nolato, and AAK.

Another common strategy, especially among the branded consumer product companies, has been to seek **consumer advantage**. This involves creating a strong brand identity and building a loyal customer base, which can provide a competitive advantage and lead to a higher gross margin. Examples of companies that have successfully implemented this strategy include Royal Unibrew, Swedish Match, and Orkla. By focusing on establishing a unique and recognizable brand, these companies have been able to differentiate themselves from competitors and attract customers who are willing to pay a premium for their products. This approach can be particularly effective in markets where there are many similar products or where consumers are highly influenced by brand reputation and loyalty.

Yet another strategy pursued is that of **differentiation,** which involves distinguishing a company's products or services from those of its competitors by offering unique features, design, quality, or customer experience. This can be achieved through investing in research and development to create innovative products, improving the design of existing products, or leveraging technology to offer better functionality or customer service. Again, we can put Atlas Copco on the list, this time along with names like Nolato, Hexpol, and Coloplast.

4. Diversification

The fourth and final major strategy that we identified for improving earnings stability was diversification. However, as we will discuss further in Chapter 6, it may conflict with the goal of achieving operational excellence and focusing on the core business. Despite this potential conflict, there are clear benefits for companies that can efficiently operate as a conglomerate, including geographic and product diversification. Some companies in our peer group that have been successful in running diversified operations include Atlas Copco, Nolato, Beijer Ref, and NIBE.

Given that Atlas Copco pursues several of the strategies listed above, it comes as no surprise that the company displays one of the lowest margin volatility ratios among our surveyed companies. We will revert to Atlas Copco in Chapter 13, where we conduct a more thorough case study about the company's business strategy and financial targets.

Methods for Achieving the Strategy Change

The main methods undertaken by the companies in order to achieve the desired strategic changes typically involve portfolio reallocation activities like acquisitions, divestments, or spin-offs.

For companies in financial and operational difficulties, the journey towards higher earnings quality often starts with **divesting non-core assets**. This has, for example, been the case in the turn-around stories of GN Store Nord and Royal Unibrew. Divestments are also very common among companies that wish to reposition themselves towards new market segments within their industry. This has been a very common strategy among the pulp and paper companies as they have exited the fine paper, pulp, and newsprint segments and focused on the less volatile and faster growing packaging segments.

Yet, another group that has managed to improve margin stability by divesting part of their business is some of the conglomerates. Orkla, Nokia, and Trelleborg, for example, chose to sell off business units that did no longer fit into the new and more streamlined business strategy.

Another route towards a stronger focus on the core business is to spin-off a business unit. This has been a popular activity among Nordic corporates, and we will explore this topic further in Chapter 6. There are plenty of examples among the list of high earnings quality companies that have applied spin-off as a strategy, such as Sandvik, Atlas Copco, and Novo Nordisk.

One strategy to achieve improved margin stability and earnings quality can, as we mentioned earlier, be through a higher aftermarket sale or a better geographic or product diversification. The fastest route to this goal is often to make various kinds of **strategic acquisitions**. In Part 2 of the book, we will delve into M&A in greater detail. At this point, it suffices to say that making acquisitions is a tool that many of our screened companies have used when trying to increase their earnings quality.

Case Study: Nolato

Our focus will now shift to Nolato, a company that has been able to increase its pricing power and reduce cyclicality through a series of successful strategic moves. Nolato is a manufacturer of polymer-based components and systems for various industries, including healthcare, automotive, telecommunications, and consumer electronics. By 2010, the company was confronted with major challenges as its traditional subcontractor role, which involved manufacturing components according to customer specifications, had reached its limits. The CEO, Christer Wahlquist, recognized that:

> *The suppliers of the future need to be able to offer customers everything from concept discussions and development support to delivery of the final product. They also need to be able to offer local production worldwide to support customers as they develop.*[2]

Nolato managed to transform itself from a regional component supplier into a global solutions provider through a wide set of strategic initiatives. Central to this transformation was a strong corporate culture that prioritized innovation, customer focus, and continuous improvement. The company demonstrated a clear commitment to investing in research and product development, which facilitated expansion of its product portfolio.

The company tried to become less dependent on the volatile and extremely competitive mobile phone market and aimed to increase exposure to the more stable and niche-oriented med-tech sector. This strategic move was highlighted by the acquisitions of British pharma packaging company Cope Allman Jaycare in 2012 and US medical technology GW Plastics in 2020.

One of the key challenges that Nolato faced was the need to shift its corporate culture from one that was focused on manufacturing to one that was more innovation-driven. To achieve this, the company began recruiting engineers and other technical experts with experience in product development and R&D. Nolato also created cross-functional teams that included members from different parts of the organization. This helped break down silos and encourage knowledge sharing and collaboration.

In general, there is a strong link between innovation and entrepreneurial spirit and having a decentralized organizational structure. This is something that Nolato understands well. Local management teams around the world have significant autonomy to lead their units independently. The role of group management is focused on setting targets,

[2] Source: Company web-page. https://www.nolato.com/en/Stories/Nolatos-strategic-transformation.

ensuring that the pace and direction are appropriate, and providing support if necessary.

Another significant factor in Nolato's turnaround was its emphasis on operational excellence and cost control. The company implemented several initiatives aimed at enhancing efficiency, which resulted in improved margins and profitability. For instance, Nolato invested in new production equipment and streamlined its manufacturing processes to decrease lead times and enhance quality.

Despite these accomplishments, Nolato still encountered substantial challenges. The company was competing against larger and more established players in the med-tech industry, which made it difficult to gain market share. To address this challenge, Nolato not only continued to invest in R&D and product development but did so with a particular focus on niche markets where it could differentiate itself from its competitors.

Nolato's transformation is an inspiring example of how a struggling company can reinvent itself through innovation, a decentralized entrepreneurial spirit, and a strong focus on customer value. By focusing on portfolio reallocation, culture, R&D, and operational excellence, Nolato was able to successfully transform itself from a regional supplier of polymer components into a global solutions provider with higher as well as more stable margins as a result.

From 2010 to 2020, the equity market rewarded Nolato shareholders with an astonishing average annual return of 32.6%. The main contributor to the total shareholder return was the increase in the valuation multiple, which accounted for almost half of the return. This increase was partly due to higher growth expectations; however, it is also a clear indicator that the equity market appreciated Nolato's improved earnings quality. Worth noting is that, as Fig. 4.3 shows, it takes time, even for a very successful story like Nolato's, before investors fully appreciate and acknowledge the company's higher earnings quality.

Earnings Quality and Shareholder Value Creation

Among the companies within our Nordic peer group that actively pursued successful strategies to improve their earnings quality, virtually all delivered a return in excess of their cost of capital. On the other hand, only a fraction of the companies that ended the period with a worse margin volatility ratio managed to achieve positive excess returns. There are, of

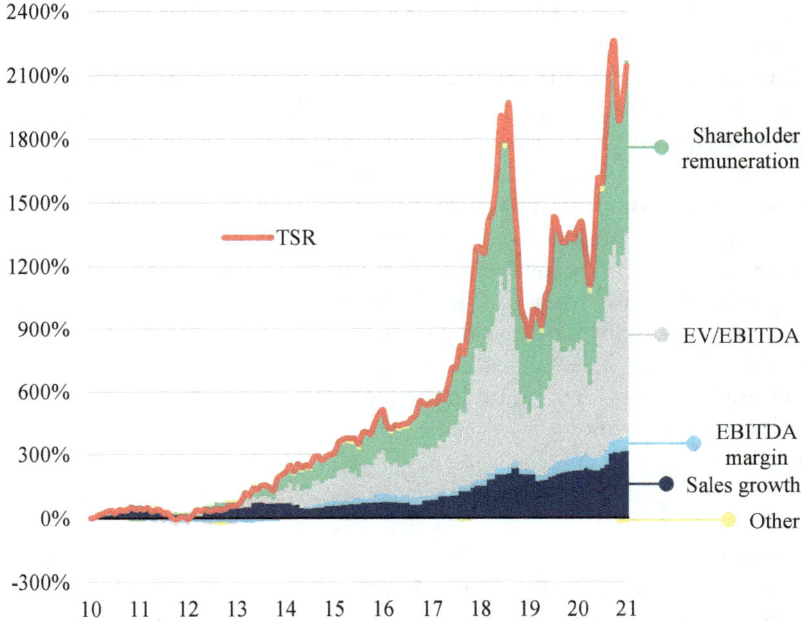

Fig. 4.3 Nolato TSR decomposition (Dec 2006–Dec 2020)

course, a wide range of factors other than just earnings quality and margin resilience that influence a company's return. Therefore, our rather limited study should be interpreted with caution. Nevertheless, improved earnings quality can be a significant and sometimes underestimated driver for shareholder value creation. However, what are, in terms of shareholder value creation, the main risks associated with strategies aimed at achieving a higher earnings quality?

One of the main challenges associated with strategies to improve earnings quality is the need to balance short-term financial pressures with long-term strategic objectives. This often goes hand in hand with the challenge to manage the expectations of stakeholders, including customers, employees, and investors. There may also be a need to manage organizational culture and ensure that employees are engaged and committed to a potentially required transformation process.

Another potential risk, particularly for companies aiming to achieve higher-quality earnings through an acquisition-based strategy, is that of overpaying for targets. This will be a topic we will further explore in the next part of the book.

However, most of the companies with deteriorated earnings quality have been unable to respond to adverse market conditions in a timely and sufficient way. Thus, the highest risk concerning margin stability may rather be linked to inertia and doing too little too late in response to changes in the competitive landscape.

Another contributing factor to ending up in the lower part of the sample is a lack of focus on earnings quality as a value driver. This is typically the case when the pursued strategy has an excessive focus on growth. In many cases, companies have paid a high price for their growth ambitions in terms of earnings quality. This can manifest itself, for example, through taking on low-quality customers or entering geopolitically unstable markets.[3]

Conclusions

In this chapter, we attempt to describe how earnings quality and margin resilience can be linked to the cost of capital and in turn shareholder value creation. It has been challenging to find academic literature investigating the relationship between earnings quality and the cost of capital, particularly with the focus that we are interested in, namely that of earnings persistency and predictability. However, our simplistic approach of using a margin volatility ratio finds support in the fact that Standard & Poor's deploys a similar line of thinking when quantitatively assessing its business risk profile.

Earnings quality often correlates with other value drivers, notably the return on invested capital, making it difficult to analyze in isolation. Despite these limitations, we can confidently conclude that improved earnings quality can have a significant impact on a firm's valuation. We also think it is fair to claim that, for too many companies, earnings quality as a value driver has not received the strategic focus it deserves.

There are several strategic approaches a company can use to improve its long-term earnings quality. By studying our sample group, we identified four categories of successfully used strategies in particular, namely:

[3] Companies with an adverse margin volatility development that during the reviewed period to some extent fit this description included Ericsson, Telia, and FL Smith.

improving operational excellence, decreasing cyclicality, and increasing the prospects of pricing power and diversification.

However, earnings stability is not as important a value driver for a high growth company as it is for a low-growth company. Moreover, not all companies succeed in their pursuit of higher margin resilience. The main risk on the journey towards higher earnings quality may include soft factors like balancing long and short-term targets as well as reshaping the company's culture.

Even with successfully implemented strategies, it often takes time before the market fully recognizes and appreciates a company's higher earnings quality. Investors need to gain confidence in the "new" or revised business model, which must prove itself to be resilient to cyclical swings and structural shifts in the marketplace. Therefore, from a management perspective, patience and faith are required to believe that the strategic direction towards improved earnings quality will eventually pay off.

Reference

Merton RC (1974) On the Pricing of Corporate Debt: The Risk Structure of Interest Rates. The Journal of Finance 29(2): 449-470

PART II

Cash Flow Deployment Alternatives

Once management has decided what value driver levers to pull and what business strategies to pursue, it is time to consider what capital allocation alternatives may take the company closer to its desired goals. In the second part of this book, we take a look at the dynamics surrounding some of the cash flow deployments alternatives that management has at its disposal.

However, before investigating the different options in more detail, we believe it is of interest to put the actual cash flow deployment in a historical context.

Cash Flow Deployment

When we study historical data from our Nordic peer group, a strong asymmetry can be observed in how companies deploy their cash flows. For example, M&A activity tends to be pro-cyclical, with companies typically carrying out deals when market liquidity is good, which coincides with a strong economy and booming stock markets. Share buyback activity follows the same pattern, albeit less pronounced, with peaks occurring when the business cycle and valuations peak.

However, cash flow allocations towards capital expenditures and, to some extent, dividends tend to be much more stable.[1]

[1] Our findings from the Nordic peer group are in line with research conducted by Mauboussin and Callahan (2022).

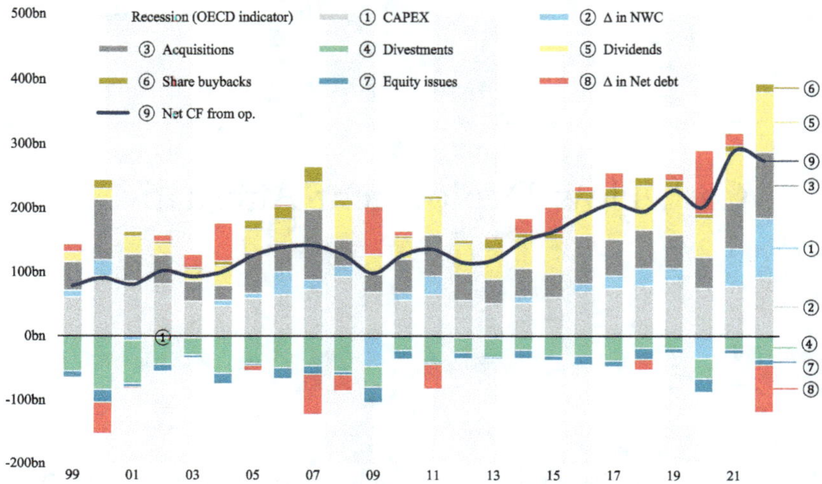

Fig. 1 Nordic cash flow deployment (1999–2022) in real value source: Capital IQ

Being pro-cyclical can apparently come with a cost. However, allocating capital relying too heavily on history might not be a good idea either. Research by McKinsey (2020) suggests that those companies that tried to avoid inertia, and hence were more proactive in reallocating resources, delivered a higher total shareholder return than the companies that took the prior year's allocation as a starting point.

The structure of This Part

We will start this part with a chapter where we examine different aspects of M&A. We will then in turn look at portfolio optimization and divestments, shareholder remunerations, capital structure, and financial risk.

Most of the chapters follow the same structure, starting by a brief review of what the academic world has to say about the topic. We then try to supplement the empirical evidence with our own peer-group study. Where applicable, we end the chapters with a "practical" check-list on the specific subject.

Compared to the US data, we observe a large difference in the pattern of shareholder remunerations. As share buybacks are still relatively uncommon in the Nordic space, we see a larger volatility in dividend pay-outs for our peer group.

References

Mauboussin MJ, CallahanD (2022) Capital Allocation—Results, Analysis and Assessment. Published online. https://www.morganstanley.com/im/publication/insights/articles/article_capitalallocation.pdf

McKinsey (2020) Divesting with agility. Published online. https://www.mckinsey.com/capabilities/strategy-and-corporate-finance/our-insights/divesting-with-agility

CHAPTER 5

The Art of Deal-Making

Mergers and Acquisitions are one of the biggest cash spends for corporates and, as such, have a significant impact on the firm's operations. Despite its widespread popularity, a substantial amount of literature demonstrates that pursuing an acquisitive strategy comes with a high risk to value creation. The wide range of expected returns suggests that executives at acquiring companies should put in extra effort to master the art of deal-making.

In this chapter, we will review strategies that are available for improving the chances of making value-creating acquisitions. We will start by looking at what academic analysis has to say about the subject. Next, we try to apply the academic lenses when we review the deals made in our Nordic sample group. We will also gain insight into how the Swedish sustainable energy company NIBE thinks about making acquisitions. We end this chapter by putting together our own version of a check-list when it comes to M&A and value creation.

What the Empirical Evidence Tells us About M&A and Value Creation

The profitability of M&A activity has generated a huge amount of academic studies during the last few decades. We will review this extensive topic with three different lenses: reviewing a meta-study, investigating

T. Arenbo, *Capital Allocation and Value Creation*,
https://doi.org/10.1007/978-3-031-47048-6_5

public versus private deals, and, finally, looking at the correlation between acquisition deal type and success probabilities.

A Meta-Study Review

We start by looking at a meta-study where Renneberg and Vansteenkiste (2019) investigate 151 studies performed after 2005, zooming in on the question: what will lead to success or failure in M&A transactions?

Once again, a broad dispersion of results emerges. Out of more than 25 investigated deal characteristics, they only identify three that prove to be consistent predictors of stock returns and operating performance. First, **serial acquisition** performance declines on the margin as the firm increases its acquisitiveness. According to evidence, this points at CEO overconfidence as the main driver of marginal underperformance. However, more factors are at play. As the firm's growth opportunity gradually diminishes, and the best acquisition opportunities are exhausted, targets may shift from small private companies to large listed ones.

Their second finding is that **related or focused acquisitions** outperform unrelated or diversifying acquisitions. This seems to be true regardless of whether the driving factor is related to product market, supply chain, technology, or human capital overlap.

Third, they conclude that deal performance is positively affected by **investor and shareholder intervention**. Evidence indicates that different kinds of shareholder activism improves stock performance as well as operating results over the longer term.

Worth noting is that no conclusive evidence could be found for factors such as method of payment, sources of financing, target financial distress, and post-merger restructuring. However, if the CEO has an equity-based compensation scheme, it generally increases stock returns. One characteristic that the study did not look into was the public versus private target dimension of acquisitions. As it was a common feature among our top performers in the Nordic sample group, we will devote some extra attention to the subject later. But first, we will see how Renneberg and Vansteenkiste summarize their findings in two general points.

The odds for a positive M&A performance are improved if:

- a company excels at **merger execution and integration** and if
- owners and board members are **actively governing** the managers

Again, given the limited number of factors that consistently predict the success or failure of M&A deals, the potential for creating value through acquisitions largely depends on the abilities of executives and board members.

Public versus Private Deals

Our second empirical lens investigates the relation between public versus private deals. As previously stated in the book, we could see a pattern in our sample where many of the top performers were involved in serial acquisitions of primarily private companies. And looking at evidence from academic studies, it seems to be no coincidence to find that the over-performing companies have been focusing on private rather than public deals. Acquiring privately held companies is an attractive option for creating shareholder value. See Draper and Paudyal (2006), Conn et al. (2005), and Rehm et al. (2012). But why is that?

Price for Private Targets is Lower Due To Size And Liquidity Discount

In financial markets, the size and liquidity of a company are crucial in determining its price. This notion was quantified by Goetz (2021) in a recent study, which found that private companies are typically valued at a 13% discount on the EBITDA multiple compared to public companies. The discount grows as the size of the target company decreases.

The size of a company also plays a role in the potential for synergies. Smaller target companies typically have less efficient and professional organizations, which leads to more opportunities for finding synergies in areas like R&D, marketing, sourcing, and logistics.

Furthermore, many of the serial acquirers we find in the top quartile of our sample are active in markets with few natural buyers and with many small potential target companies. This kind of supply/demand dynamics limits the prospects of auction processes, and the buyer gets the upper hand in the price negotiations.

Preferred Buyer

Another instance where auctions are avoided is when the acquiring firm is regarded as the preferred buyer. Based on our experiences, this is more common when the selling company places more emphasis on the buyer's qualities rather than just the price. This may happen when a business founder is selling and wants to ensure that the company's legacy is in good hands. The preferred buyer usually has a decentralized structure that preserves the target company's brand, employees, and culture. Additionally, the buyer must be able to provide the selling company with the necessary capital and expertise to grow their business.

Public Deals Are More Risky
Public deals tend to be larger and thus more risky for the acquirer in terms of timing. This is especially true as M&A activity is pro-cyclical, and most transactions occur when prices are high. Serial buyers of private firms can more easily spread their acquisitions throughout the cycle. Since public companies are always to some extent up for sale, it is impossible to avoid the auction process when purchasing the entire company. To do so, a significant premium must be paid on top of the current market price, which is usually a good indicator of the company's true value. The higher the premium, the greater the synergies must be to make the acquisition economically justified.

Probability of M&A Success Based on Deal Type

Our third and last way of approaching empirical evidence and M&A is by looking at it with the categorization developed by Clark and Mills (2013). The authors build upon prior research about size and business relatedness when they establish four categories divided into nine different sub-types of acquisitions. For each type, they estimate a "deal success probability range". The four categories and their subcategories are: **Opportunistic** (Bottom-trawlers), **Operational** (Bolt-ons, Line-extension equivalents, Multiple core-related complementary, Single core-related complementary), **Transitional** (Consolidation–mature, Consolidation–emerging), and **Transformational** (Lynchpin strategic, Speculative strategic). The top-ranked type of acquisition is the bottom-trawlers with an estimated success rate of 87–92% followed by Bolt-ons (80–85%). At the lower end of the scale, the two types of transformational acquisitions are found where success-rate probabilities are estimated to be around 20%

The success probability rates presented by the authors are their own evaluations based on certain assumptions regarding industries and bid premiums and should be considered as suggestive only. Nonetheless, it is worth highlighting the significant disparity in success rates between bottom-trawlers and bolt-ons and the two transformative types of deals.

Their methodology is highly useful in determining the value creation probabilities for various types of deals, making it easily accessible for shareholders and boards attempting to assess the value at risk for a proposed transaction.

Reviewing our Nordic Peer Group from an M&A Perspective

Value creation and M&A are often closely tied to the issue of determining the most suitable owner of the business. Our Nordic study data suggest that there is a correlation between a company's operational performance and M&A success. Although it is evident that factors other than the deals themselves have impacted excess returns during the time period analyzed, the data still suggest that M&A-intensive companies with high ROIC spreads outperform less M&A-intensive companies with the same ROIC spreads. However, the difference between the two M&A groups disappears when the ROIC spread approaches zero.[1] The data not only supports the value creation formula, but also adds to our firm belief that in order to be "the best owner" of a business you need to start by having your own house in order. And this belief finds support in the academic research. See for example Qian and Zhu (2018).

Size Seems to Matter a Great Deal

When we screen our Nordic sample group for private versus public deals, we find a remarkable large number of serial acquirers of relatively small **privately owned companies** among the top performers. The acquiring companies are concentrated to three different groups; service companies (Sweco, ÅF, Knowit, Etteplan, Reijlers), industrial consolidators (BeijerRef, NIBE, Addnode, DSV, Proact, Per Aarsleff, Assa Abloy), and investment companies (Indutrade, Addtech, OEM, Schouw). Out of the 16 companies mentioned above, 13 belong to the top quartile and the rest to the second best quartile.

These companies share several characteristics when it comes to creating value in private deals. They typically have a *long-term acquisition strategy*,

[1] The number of companies doing M&A with a negative ROIC spread is too small to draw any conclusions from.

a *deep understanding of their sector*, and focus their acquisitions on targets within the *same industry*. In some cases, the buyer has established a strong reputation as an acquirer and is considered the *preferred buyer* for *privately owned companies*. These companies also often have a decentralized organization that allows local management to benefit from the advantages of a larger parent company, in areas such as supply management, funding, and sales organization. Additionally, price may not always be the top priority for the seller and other factors, such as the legacy of their firm, may take precedence. Furthermore, many of the target companies in this group are too small to be sold through an IPO, and auction processes may be avoided.

Nearly all companies in this group have grown with a positive ROIC spread (even though the trend in profitability often is slightly downward sloping which ties well into the earlier point from the meta-study about decreasing marginal value creation for serial acquirers).

Acquisitions turn out to be a relatively large group for the bottom performers as well. Maybe it does not come as a surprise that in this category we see a different kind of M&As compared to the top performers. Companies like Sanoma and Elanders made acquisitions in order to boost growth outside their slow-growing domestic market. Some other companies made **large public deals**, like for example when the Swedish steel company SSAB bought the Canadian peer company IPSCO right before the global financial crisis. Large acquisitions outside your home markets seem to be a recipe for low returns. To that list, we can add Carlsberg's acquisition of Russian BBH as well as Telia's emerging market endeavours.

ITAB, Lindab, Husqvarna, and, as mentioned, SSAB are examples of companies with low returns that all made acquisitions leading to a materially higher operational as well as financial risk. Coupled with poor market timing, this turned out to be a toxic combination for the valuation of the companies.

That being said, is it accurate to conclude that only serial acquirers of private companies are successful in purchasing companies? Real life is more complex than that. There have been several successful acquisitions of large, publicly traded companies, even in new markets, such as Atlas Copco's acquisition of British Edwards Group and Assa Abloy's purchase of Swedish Cardo. Unlike some of the less successful buyers, these two companies had a much higher pre-merger profitability. A more accurate conclusion about large acquisitions would rather be that some types of

M&A activities come with a significant risk to value creation. These findings suggested by our limited study probably come as no surprise. The subject of M&A and value creation has, as we have seen, been thoroughly studied with results being just as unambiguous as those we see in our study.

The Nordic Sample According to the Clark and Mills Categorisation

In this part, we have screened our sample for high M&A activity and selected the companies with the highest share of cash flow devoted to acquisitions. We categorize their acquisitions or acquisition strategies according to the Clark and Mills deal types. Due to the relatively low numbers of observations, we have reduced the number of categories. We merged Single and Multi-core related complementary into one category and did the same with the two separate consolidation types. Furthermore, we did not identify any candidates for the "Bottom-trawler" category. We try to assess the success of the respective M&A activities by evaluating four criteria: *the operational performance*, *the share price performance*, *equity analyst comments*, and *company comments about realized synergies versus the bid premium.*[2] Sometimes this is no easy task given the complexity of the transactions and the limited information disclosed for the acquired entities. Nonetheless, in aggregate, our assessments of the deals probably give a fairly adequate picture of the "true" success rate. Our result resembles to a relative large extent the success probabilities presented by Clarks and Mills.

The most common deal type turns out to be the **bolt-on acquisition** strategy with 11 companies represented. Our group of Nordic companies confirms Clark and Mills expected high success rate at around 90%. The variability in success rates among the group is relatively low, and all companies are able to maintain a positive ROIC spread. Companies in this group include Beijer Ref, Addtech, and Assa Abloy as well as several consulting firms. Transactions are usually spread out over a period of time and are limited in size, except for occasional platform acquisitions.

The second most common type of deal is the so-called **line extension equivalent** and, according to Clark and Mills, we would expect the group to display a fairly high success rate (67%). However, our numbers struggle

[2] Some of the companies appear twice as they, for example, can have pursued a bolt-on acquisition strategy as well as have made larger acquisitions.

to meet the levels expected. When we dig into the material a common denominator among the laggards reveals itself—expansion outside the core geographic markets. Here we find Carlsberg's acquisition of Russian BBH and Telia's (and to some extent also Telenor's) emerging market adventures. On the other hand, Elekta's, and in particular Hexagon's and GN Store Nord's, tech and software related complimentary acquisitions are an example of value-creating acquisition strategies in this category.

When it comes to the two types of **consolidation** strategies, there is a notable increase in deal size, and the transactions are often cross border or even cross continental. Again, our assessment of the success rate varies a lot within the group. On the one hand, we have the great synergy story of Kongsbergs Gruppen and the acquisition of Rolls Royce CM. On the other hand, we have deals like Trelleborg and their acquisition of Czech CGS which we deem value destroying. As previously mentioned, SSAB's merger with IPSCO also falls into this category, highlighting the significant timing risk involved in large transactions. Overall, our estimated success rate stays at a relatively modest 50%.

Another significant group of deals falls under the category of "**core-related complimentary**". This category encompasses nine deals, including Schibsted's strategy to penetrate the online classified market. Other examples of deals in this group include Elekta's acquisition of Nucletron and Assa Abloy's merger with Cardo. The success rate in this group (on average 50%) varies greatly, with some underperforming deals like FLSmith's acquisition of Decanter and others that have added great value to the company, such as Royal Unibrew.

The fifth and last group of transactions, the **transformational**, is sparsely populated. We have classified Sanoma's merger with SBS and Elander's strategy to enter the logistics industry as well as Telia's acquisition of TV4 in this group. The former has been a distinct value destroyer. Elander's strategy change has yielded very low operating returns, however with a rather strong share price performance. In the Telia case, the jury is still out, though we would deem the odds for success as very low.

Notable is that we have not been able to spot any opportunistic type of mergers among our screened sample.

Synergies—The Key to Unlock Value

It has been established that mergers and acquisitions in aggregate generally generate value. However, for the acquiring party, the question is whether the synergies surpass the target bid premium. Unfortunately, realizing synergies seems to be much more challenging than projecting them.

Synergies are typically split up into cost and revenue synergies. Cost synergies include, for example, a reduction in overhead costs or improved purchasing power. Other examples of cost synergies can be consolidating overlapping operations and streamlining supply chains. Common revenue synergies may include cross-selling opportunities, positive network effects, increased pricing power, and better geographical market reach.

Data from Deloitte's Synergy database show that synergies vary greatly by company and deal. The top quartile unlocks synergies of almost four times as much as the lowest quartile.[3]

In order to find out if a transaction is likely to be value creating, you need to calculate the present value of the estimated synergies (post tax). We typically use the perpetuity formula and divide the estimated synergies post tax with the cost of capital for the acquiring firm. If, for example, the estimated synergies are EUR 100m, a tax rate of 21%, and a cost of capital of 8%, we reach a present value of the synergies of: (100*0.79) / 0.08 = 987.5m This is the number that should exceed the target bid premium.

In theory, this is a rather straightforward calculation but, given the poor evidence for the buyers' ability to create value from M&A, executives seem to be on thin ice when it comes to estimating and realizing synergies. And to no surprise, academic literature suggests that synergies are often overestimated and difficult to achieve, with three common pitfalls being the "mirage" (overestimation of synergy potential), the "gravity hill" (underestimation of difficulties in realizing synergies), and "amnesia" (lack of attention to realizing synergies).

This is a hot topic not only for academic researchers, but also among management consulting firms as well. Deloitte (2020), for example, has looked at a broad dataset from over 800 global transactions and,

[3] 8.4% of the deal value for the top quartile, compared to 2.2% of the lower quartile.

according to the data, roughly half of the companies announced synergies between 1 and 5% of total costs, one quarter achieved less than 1% and the best quarter achieved 5% or more.

A Bain & Company (see Miles et al. 2014) survey of 352 global executives found that overestimating synergies was the second most common reason for underperforming deals, with failed due diligence being the most common. The survey analyzed data from 22,000 companies and found that, on average, 70% of companies announced higher synergy estimates than expected based on the industry's scale curve. The Telecom and Media & Entertainment sectors had the most realistic expectations of cost synergies, while the banking industry had the least.

McKinsey (2004) found that the greatest errors in estimating synergies occur on the revenue side. Nearly 70% of the acquisitions in their sample failed to deliver the expected additional revenue. The two main reasons mentioned were a lack of outside perspective (overestimation of growth compared to the overall market) and underestimation of customer losses due to integration challenges. However, the skills of estimating cost synergies were found to be better, with almost 90% of the sample achieving 70% or more of their expectations. This is because cost synergies are mostly within the control of the business itself, while revenue synergies are influenced by external factors such as customer and competitor response.

How to Pay for an Acquisition

Companies making acquisitions often inform the market whether the deal is EPS accretive or not. This has very little to do with whether the deal is value crating or not. It takes a really poor performance for an acquisition funded with cheap debt not to be EPS accretive. However, an exclusive focus on EPS fails to take into account the increased return on equity requirements that result from higher leverage. More importantly, an EPS focus fails to provide information on whether the deal is accretive or dilutive in terms of intrinsic business value. By now, we know that the true value drivers are not short-term EPS but long-term growth, ROIC and cost of capital.

The source of financing for acquisitions also deserves some consideration. Research suggests that the market tends to prefer deals that are financed with cash rather than equity. One way to pay for an acquisition using stock is to issue new equity to the market and use the proceeds for the transaction. This method leaves the buyer with all of the risk. Alternatively, new stock can be issued and given to the seller as part of the payment. In this case, the buyer and the seller share some of the risk.

But if a company chooses to pay with equity, it trades part of its own value for the part of the acquired firm. Thus it becomes a relative game of valuation. This, in our view, is not always well understood by acquiring firms. It can, for example, still be value accretive for the buyer to make a stock-deal even if the target company trades at a higher multiple. Thus a stock-deal requires the acquirer not only to be aware of the intrinsic value of the target, but also have a deep understanding of the intrinsic value of their own company. In that sense, a cash bid is easier, as cash always is valued at its intrinsic value. See Cunningham (2013) page 205ff. However, a 100% cash bid assumes there is enough room for taking up debt on the balance sheet.

If we assume that both the acquiring company and the target company are fairly valued, the decision about using equity or not can be reduced to two questions. The first question concerns the desired financial risk level after the acquisition. The second question involves the risk associated with realizing synergies versus overpaying. The more confident the acquiring company is about creating value through the deal, the larger the cash component of the payment should be.

How we at NIBE think about making acquisitions

By Gerteric Lindquist, Managing Director and CEO NIBE and Hans Backman, CFO NIBE

At NIBE, our investment strategy revolves around acquiring companies that align with our core values and contribute to our sustainable energy solutions portfolio. Our acquisition strategy aims at expanding our product offerings, enter new markets, and enhance our position as a leader in the industry.

We mostly pursue bolt-on acquisitions which involve acquiring smaller or mid-size companies that complement our existing product portfolio. Larger companies are also occasionally acquired. Such companies have allowed us to quicker enter new geographies or strengthen our market position in existing markets. To date, we have completed a significant number of acquisitions, totalling over 150 acquisitions spanning over a period of some 30 years.

We seek businesses that share our customer-centric approach and commitment to innovation and sustainability. An engaged and entrepreneurially oriented local management team is key. Cultural fit is very important to us, and we want to get a good feel for the soul of the company. How are you welcomed in the reception? Are the toilets clean? Are you allowed to meet and chat with the employees? And what are the thoughts about the future and product development? All of these are small puzzle pieces that ultimately determine if the companies culturally fit into NIBE.

Being a "preferred buyer" is another important aspect of our acquisition strategy. We strive to establish a reputation as a preferred partner for companies looking to be acquired. This means building trust, maintaining open communication, and demonstrating our commitment to achieving a collaborative and supportive environment for acquired companies where both parties can benefit from each other. By being a preferred buyer, we aim to attract businesses that align with our values and goals, creating mutually beneficial partnerships.

Linking to the point of being a preferred buyer, an important cornerstone in our acquisition strategy is to maintain a decentralized organizational structure. Acquired companies are encouraged to continue to operate as legal entities with existing management and under their existing brand names with a high level of autonomy. This approach allows us to benefit from the entrepreneurial spirit and expertise of our acquired companies while achieving a collaborative environment within NIBE.

In general, we strive to acquire companies that are profitable, have a strong and entrepreneurial management, have survived economic downturns, and have not changed ownership too frequently. In most cases, that means staying away from turn-around cases as well as being cautious buying from Private Equity firms.

Note: NIBE is a global group that develops and manufactures energy-efficient indoor comfort solutions for all types of properties. The company also supplies components and solutions for heating and control for industry and infrastructure. NIBE, with approximately 21,000 employees, achieved a turnover of over EUR 4 billion in 2022.

Conclusions

In theory, it is rather straightforward to calculate the expected value of an acquisition. But in real life, it proves to be hard to do successful acquisitions where potential pitfalls may include overpaying, a too optimistic view on synergies and poor integration. A study performed by Graham et al. (2013) finds evidence that links CEOs psychological traits such as risk-aversion and optimism to corporate activities like acquisitions. Especially, if the deal is more dependent on realizing revenue synergies and is transformational in nature, it implies a higher risk to value creation.

How can managers bring down the risk of doing value-destroying acquisitions, and how can investors be better at spotting them? We have put together our own version of a check-list in order to make sure value creation prospects are in the acquirer's favour:

Best owner and competitive advantage

- Acquisitions are not inherently good or bad, but successful acquisitions emanate from a sound strategic and operational performance visible in a positive ROIC versus cost of capital spread.
- Is the company a leader in its industry? (And is the industry attractive enough for making acquisitions? - see point above)
- Does it have experience in doing acquisitions?
- Conducting a thorough due diligence process is critical to identifying potential risks and synergies associated with the target company. A company also needs to have the necessary integration capabilities in order to realize the expected synergies.

Price versus value

- Small versus large

Smaller companies typically have fewer options available when the owners want to sell the company, which affects the negotiation power negatively.

- Public vs private

  Academic studies seem to be rather consistent when it comes to acquisitions of non-public firm being value accretive. There are some reasons why this seems plausible, including the lack of liquidity and transparency in a private company compared to a public company, which affects the price negatively. In addition, a private company might be acquired without having an auction process and without having to negotiate with a large number of shareholders.
- Preferred buyer

  Many owners care about the legacy of their business they are about to sell. The preferred buyer usually has a decentralized structure and is able to provide the selling company with the necessary capital and expertise to grow their business.
- Timing

  There is evidence to suggest that acquisition activities are procyclical and tend to increase during periods of economic growth and stability. During such periods, acquirers are typically willing to pay higher prices for the targets as they have more resources and are more confident about the future.

Type of acquisition

- To what extent and how can the acquisition improve the performance of the combined company?

  There are several potential strategies that may improve the performance of the combined company, including: improving operational efficiency, leveraging technology and innovation as well as marketing and branding optimization.
- Revenue or cost synergies?

  In general revenue and strategic synergies tend to be the most challenging to achieve but also have the greatest potential to create long-term value. Cost and financial synergies tend to be more achievable but may not create as much long-term value.
- Strategic coherence

Strategic coherence ensures that the acquisition is aligned with the acquirer's overall strategy and goals. It helps the acquirer to mitigate risks, enhance integration efforts, avoid distractions, and communicate effectively with stakeholders.

- Cultural fit

  A successful acquirer considers the cultural fit between the two companies. A lack of cultural alignment might lead to integration challenges. Thus it is important that the acquiring firm understands and respects the target company's culture and values and has a plan to address any potential cultural differences.
- Deal type

  As a final check the proposed acquisition could be evaluated through the lens of Clark and Mills' deal types; Opportunistic (Bottom-trawlers), Operational (Bolt-ons, Line-extension equivalents, Multiple core-related complementary, Single core-related complementary), Transitional (Consolidation–mature, Consolidation–emerging), and Transformational (Lynchpin strategic, Speculative strategic).

References

Clark PJ, Mills RW (2013) Masterminding the Deal: Breakthroughs in M&A Strategy and Analysis, Kogan Page (Chapter 4)

Conn RL, Cosh A, Guest PM, Hughes A (2005) The Impact on UK Acquirers of Domestic, Cross-border, Public and Private Acquisitions. Journal of Business Finance & Accounting 32(5–6): 815–870

Cunningham LA (2013) The Essays of Warren Buffet—Lessons for Corporate America. Carolina Academic Press, Third edition (p. 205ff)

Deloitte (2020) Unlocking the Full Potential of M&A—What it Takes to Be a Value Creation Champion. ch-en-fa-st-gallen-mergers-acquisitions-study-v2.pdf (deloitte.com)

Draper P, Paudyal K (2006) Acquisitions: Private versus Public. European Financial Management 12(1): 57–80

Goetz S (2021) Public versus Private: New Insights into the Private Company Discount. Journal of Business Valuation and Economic Loss Analysis 16(1): 15–40.

Graham JR, Harvey CR, Puri M (2013) Managerial Attitudes and Corporate Actions. Journal of Financial Economics (109): 103–121

McKinsey (2004) Where Mergers Go Wrong. McKinsey on Finance 10: 1–7

Miles L, Borchert A, Ramanathan AE (2014) Why Some Merging Companies Become Synergy Overachievers. Bain & Company

Qian J, Lei Zhu J (2018) Return to Invested Capital and the Performance of Mergers Acquisiitons. Management Science 64(10): 4818–4834

Rehm W, Uhlaner R, West A (2012) Taking a Longer-term Look at M&A Value Creation. McKinsey Quarterly

Renneboog L, Vansteenkiste C (2019) Failure and Success in Mergers and Acquisitions. CentER Discussion Paper Series No. 2019–026

CHAPTER 6

Portfolio Optimisation and Why Less So Often Is More

Not all investments or acquisitions succeed. How should management evaluate investments that do not reach their expected returns? Should the assets be divested or should attempts be made to turn the underperforming entity around? A key factor in a successful long-term capital allocation process is a continuous re-evaluation of the business portfolio to determine which assets to keep and why.

When management makes decisions about which operations to pursue or not pursue, some important questions must be asked: Are the assets crucial to the firm's core businesses? Would the firm purchase these assets today if given the choice? What is an appropriate value, and is the firm the best owner of the operations? An investment may not earn its cost of capital due to poor management execution or changing industry dynamics, such as off-shoring trends, technological changes, or new competitors entering the industry.

A sound capital allocation process includes estimating the value of the assets under their current ownership and comparing it to what it might be worth to other owners. After reading about the relatively poor odds of making acquisitions that are value creating, it should come as no surprise that the opposite is true for divestitures. In a meta-analysis of the divestiture performance, encompassing 94 studies, the results indicate that corporate divestiture positively impacts subsequent performance. See

T. Arenbo, *Capital Allocation and Value Creation*,
https://doi.org/10.1007/978-3-031-47048-6_6

Lee and Madhavan (2010). These observations have support from the equity markets as well. Between 2003 and 2022, the Bloomberg spin-off index had a yearly total return of 13.0% compared to the S&P 500 Index of 9.8%. Thus it might be management time well spent to regularly ask the question about who is the best owner of a business. And looking at company data, this seems to be a prioritized activity among corporates. In addition to pure asset sales around 50 spin-offs have taken place in the Nordic region in the last 20 years.

The Investor's Take On What to Keep and What to Divest

There is no denying that divestitures, on the whole, have generated value for shareholders. However, before making a decision on an asset sale or spin-off, it is crucial to perform a thorough cost–benefit analysis. The management should adopt an investor's perspective when evaluating the company's portfolio holdings, determining whether it is a core part of the business or if it would be more valuable in the hands of another owner. To accomplish this, BCG (2016) recommends evaluating each business from three different angles.

The first concerns *business strategy* and the potential for each business in the portfolio in terms of competitive market position. As a complement to the classical strategic review, an analysis of the relative *valuation* of each business and their potential TSR drivers should be conducted. Would the business be worth more if the value is made visible to the "right" investors? Having a clear investment thesis is crucial when a company wants to attract long-term owners who are interested in the company and its value-creating characteristics, such as differences in capital intensity, cyclicality, dividend pay-out policy, growth ambitions, operational risk appetite, and financial leverage. Finally, BCG suggests incorporating an *ownership perspective* to the analysis in order to include portfolio dynamics like operational and strategic synergies between the operations owned.

Not Always a Conglomerate Discount

Market data have historically indicated that 50–60% of conglomerates trade with a discount. This typically happens if investors view the conglomerates as less focused and less efficient than more streamlined companies.

However, some conglomerates actually trade with a premium. BCG (2017) has investigated what makes these companies successful where others tend to fail. They conclude that two common characteristics drive their performance; a *consistent business model* and a "*no excuse*" *culture of accountability*.

This is facilitated if a company builds an operating model with businesses that address their strategy consistently, or put differently, to run businesses that outperform in similar ways. In businesses that have the same culture and are run in more or less the same way, managers can move from one business unit within the company to the next fairly seamlessly. Often, and maybe somewhat counterintuitively, this seems to be the case in strongly decentralized organization with a very high accountability when it comes to growth and profitability targets.[1]

Multiple Drivers Behind Divestiture's Operational Success and Failures

Why is less so often more when it comes to divestitures and value creation? We believe that the market generally is much better at allocating capital than corporate managers. **Capital allocation** mistakes are among the most common ways for companies to destroy value. In practice, it typically takes place through a capital allocation process dictated by factors like a business unit's market share or relative size of the total company turnover. Research also shows that pure inertia, where the inherited levels of investments are carried forward without being questioned, plays an important role in capital misallocation. There is no guarantee that these types of decision variables correlate with the true value drivers. If this is the case, not only will it lead to suboptimal capital allocation but likely also to misaligned KPIs and incentives.

A second reason why less may be more can be found in the **operational and strategic focus**. For example, a large body of research shows that both the parent company and the spun-off business, on average, improve their operating margins after the demerger. Gains from increased focus can come in many forms; one such example often mentioned is increased employee engagement due to a lower vertical distance between

[1] Examples of Nordic companies with a decentralized set-up includes Assa Abloy, Atlas Copco, Wärtsilä and NIBE

management and employees in a smaller organization. Engagement from managers and employees can be further underpinned by the stronger link between their actions and the direct effect it can have on shareholder value creation and stock price. Our case study of Novo Nordisk and Novozymes will illustrate how strategic flexibility can contribute to value creation, showing how strategic alliances with customers can improve growth prospects for a spun-off company.

A third reason, tightly connected to the prior one, as to why divestitures tend to bring value to the table is related to the **scarcity of management time** and the limitations it can bring. One explanation often mentioned in this context is inadequate managerial skills for running the activities outside of the firm's core business. Moreover, management can spend too much time focusing on underperforming units rather than on developing the businesses where the majority of the value is created. Research conducted by EY (2019) highlights this issue, as it indicates that 63% of the executives say that they held onto assets too long when they should have divested them.

However, as our study of 45 Nordic spin-offs will show, there is a large dispersion between successful and less successful spin-offs. A positive outcome from a divestiture is by no means guaranteed and, for firms announcing separations, it is of great importance to have a clear plan with a credible execution strategy in place. The potential **costs of divestments** can, for example, include lost synergies that can result in higher procurement and SG&A costs. Examples of such costs could be if products and services are bundled or if products are sold by a common sales force. Other potential costs, especially for the spun-off entity, can be related to the funding where both equity and debt can come at a higher price. Furthermore, a spin-off only makes sense if the spun-off company has a sufficiently strong core business to build upon as a stand-alone entity. If that is not the case, a trade-sale would likely be a better divestiture option.

Different Ways to Divest a Business Unit

Once the decision to divest a business unit is made, there are several alternative exit routes. In an asset sale (or a so-called trade-sale) the operations are sold in an M&A transaction to a strategic or financial investor. Another way to divest the business unit is through an IPO which is targeted to equity market investors. In a spin-off, 100% of the shares in the spun-off company are listed on a stock exchange and distributed to the shareholders of the parent company.

Private transactions, like an asset sale, are typically preferable if the parent company needs immediate cash and if it is evident that there are other owners that are better equipped to run the business. In the most common type of public transaction, the spin-off, there is no cash proceeds to the parent company. Public transactions typically occur if no clear "better owner" is identified, or if the newly floated company has long-term strategic advantages as a stand-alone listed company.

In a spin-off, there is no retained ownership for the parent company, whereas a limited ownership is possible in an asset sale. In an IPO, it is typically viewed as a positive factor if the parent company remains as an owner, at least initially. The execution risk from a pricing perspective is significantly reduced in a spin-off transaction compared to the other two alternatives. As it is the least risky alternative for management and boards when it comes to timing and pricing risk, it might not be so surprising that many spun-off entities are subsequently acquired and de-listed. The spin-off can, in that sense, sometimes be seen as the first step in a potential asset sale process.

The rest of this chapter will be devoted to spin-offs and our study of 45 Nordic spin-offs taking place between 1994 and 2019.

Study Review—Nordic Spin-Offs

The study investigates the performance and TSR drivers of the spun-off entities as well as the remaining companies (RemainCo) for a period of three years starting at the date of the de-merger announcement.

Strong Performance on Average But with a Wide Dispersion

Our results firmly support earlier empirical studies concerning the strong performance of spin-offs in general. However, our findings also indicate that success is far from a guaranteed outcome. Three years after the demerger, the average outperformance for the spun-off entity is an impressive 34%. Nonetheless, the strong average performance is influenced by a handful of outliers, and the median outperformance is more modest at 13%. It turns out that more than one-third of the spun-off entities underperformed the broader market index. Additionally, it is worth

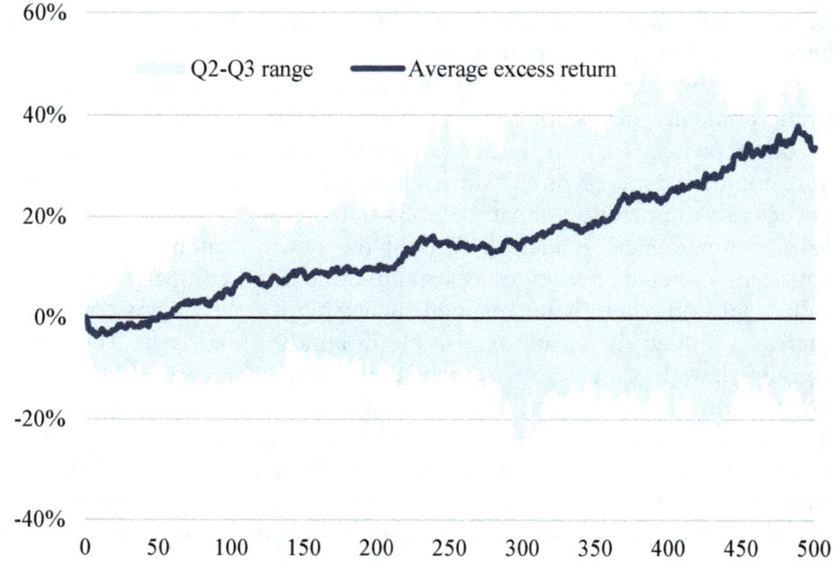

Fig. 6.1 Average excess TSR SpinCo

noting that the initial share price performance is burdened by rotation in the shareholder base, especially if SpinCo is a small part (Fig. 6.1).

The corresponding numbers for the RemainCos are along the same line, albeit at a more modest level. On average, the RemainCo outperformed the market by around 20%, with a somewhat lower dispersion of results.

TSR Drivers for the Various Groups

The wide range of results raises the question of what the drivers of performance look like. For the SpinCos, we would expect to see some margin pressure due to the presumed dis-synergies. It is also plausible to anticipate a higher multiple, thanks to a more tailored investment story and improved prospects for capital allocation. Lastly, although somewhat challenging to assess, we expect a positive effect from the potentially higher growth rate resulting from a more decentralized and "entrepreneurial" culture. Figure 6.2 shows that for the two-thirds of the sample that exceeds the "required return" of 8%, the hypotheses surrounding increased growth, and particularly multiple expansion, hold true. However, we do not see any signs of dis-synergies occurring.

We believe that several of the outperforming SpinCos have benefited, in particular from an improved strategic focus. It is also evident that unlocking the hidden value of undervalued businesses, visible as a multiple expansion in Fig. 6.2, has been a strong performance driver for several companies. However, the strongest spin-off performers differentiate themselves from the rest by having considerably stronger growth rates. This was, for instance, the case when the business-to-consumer gambling company Unibet spun off its business-to-business division, Kambi Group. The spin-off represented a strategic decision to enhance the growth prospects and market opportunities for both companies by leveraging their respective strengths in the rapidly evolving gaming industry. Henrik Tjärnström (2014), CEO of Unibet at the time, expressed it as follows:

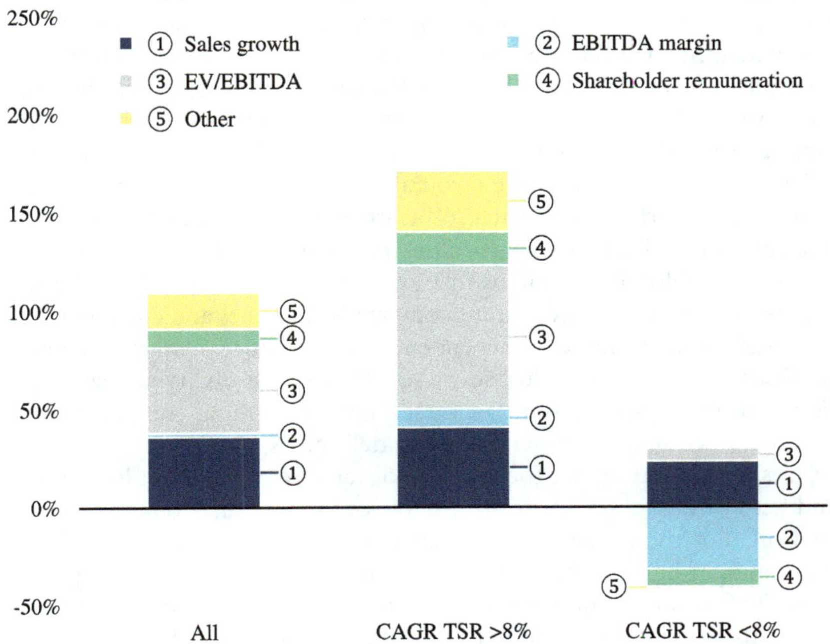

Fig. 6.2 TSR decomposition SpinCo (3 years)

> …*Unibet has focused its business on excellence in customer relationship management, while Kambi has been able to concentrate on development of its market-leading sports betting services. While Kambi has an excellent offering, its opportunity to maximise the value of those services is limited while it is under the ownership of Unibet. Separation will make it easier for Kambi to access wider markets.*

In addition to the organic growth driver of performance, several companies in our sample demonstrate a remarkably successful acquisition strategy following their spin-off. One notable example is Hexpol, which was spun off from Hexagon in 2008, and another is Assa, which de-merged from Securitas in 1994. Both companies leveraged acquisitions as a key element of their growth plans, contributing significantly to their post-spin-off success.

The underperforming part of the sample struggled with profitability. One impediment to improving profit might be if the RemainCo and/or SpinCo are too highly leveraged. We believe, for example, that was the case when the med-tech company Getinge announced to spin-off its Arjo division in 2016. Without sufficient financial resources, it may be difficult to invest enough in R&D, marketing, or machinery. Subsequently, Getinge carried out a rights issue of SEK 4bn in 2017 to strengthen the balance sheet and create more favourable conditions for the operations.

The underperformance can also be attributed to lack of having a clear strategic focus, leading to difficulties in identifying growth opportunities and establishing a unique market position. Additionally, excessive dependence on the former parent company's resources and customer base hindered some SpinCos' independence. Competitive market dynamics, particularly in mature industries, also affected the ability to gain traction and market share. Some of these underperforming companies were eventually acquired by larger firms and delisted as a result.

It is worth noting that the majority of value remains in the RemainCo, and here we can observe a relative stable outperformance on average post spin-off. For the outperforming RemainCos, two key drivers stand out. First, margin improvement plays a very important role in boosting their TSR. By focusing on optimizing operational efficiencies and cost management, these companies are able to enhance their profitability. Second, robust sales growth contributes to their outperformance, though it is at a lower level compared to the outperforming SpinCos. However, unlike the SpinCos, multiple expansion is not a significant factor driving the performance of the outperforming RemainCos. The underperforming RemainCos, on the other hand, did so primarily due to sluggish growth rates and poor margin development.

Case Study: Novo Nordisk and Novozymes

In the year 2000, the healthcare company Novo Nordisk made the decision to spin-off its enzyme business, Novozymes. A few years prior to the spin-off, Novo Nordisk had announced a business strategy that put a lot of emphasis on its businesses having enough flexibility in order to position themselves as the best business within their respective industry. The companies have much in common when it comes to the technological base, the production process, and to some extent also the sourcing of equipment and raw materials. However, their respective customers differ materially as Novo Nordisk can be categorized as business-to-consumer company while Novozymes only serves large business clients. In addition to the differences in marketing and logistics, the two industries differ in the dynamics around R&D and product development.

When it comes to the potential gains from a spin-off of Novozymes, they include (see Leimann, 2009):

- Increased strategic flexibility—with decentralized decision-making and better conditions to implement their differentiation strategy
- Increased potential for strategic alliances with core customers such as Procter & Gamble and Unilever
- Improved incentive structure for management—with the possibility of implementing share-based programmes
- Reduced asymmetrical information for investors—resulting in improved transparency
- Investors gain access to a pure exposure to an enzyme business

So how did it play out for Novozymes as a stand-alone company? For a spun-off company, it often takes some time before operational and strategic changes become visible in the accounting numbers and for the investor community. And still, three years after being spun-off the share price had barely moved. However, that was dramatically changed during the four years that followed, and when we summarize Novozymes first seven years as a stand-alone company, the annual TSR shows an impressive

23%. By opening the hood to the return engine we can get a better feel for what the share price drivers looked like. That, in turn, can reveal what strategic strings management decided to pull. It turns out that **margin** was stable during the period, i.e. any dis-synergies from the split were offset by other costs being lower. But even though the margin did not change, there was strong improvement in the **profitability** (ROIC) which primarily was driven by a higher asset turnover. That might be a bit surprising, since the main assumed synergy between Novo Nordisk and Novozymes was related to the production process. Almost a quarter of the TSR performance was attributed to a strong **sales growth** (CAGR of almost 6%). The single largest driver, however, was related to the investor perception of Novozymes and the fact that the equity market traded the stock at a **multiple** almost twice as high compared to the initial level at the listing.[2] The remaining TSR contribution stemmed from the shareholder remuneration activities, more specifically the strong return from the **share buyback activities** that took place early in the period.

The strong performance of both Novo Nordisk and Novozymes has continued well beyond the period we reviewed. This case study demonstrates that much more value can be created through reduced agency costs and increased strategic flexibility, compared to the potential loss of value stemming from potential dis-synergies.

Conclusions

The question about the value creation prospects of staying together or splitting up revolves around whether the value of **synergies** is bigger than the value of reduced **agency costs** and improved **strategic and operational flexibility**. When it comes to the first part, we can conclude that realizing synergies between business units seems to be harder than many corporate executives expect. When considering the reduction of agency costs, spin-offs result in the creation of smaller and less complex companies. This can lead to a more accurate valuation of the firm and a better aligned shareholder base. The decrease in agency costs may also result in improved capital allocation, as the financial goals and managerial incentives are better aligned with the drivers of shareholder value.

[2] The overall market multiple traded sideways during the same period.

Additionally, shareholder value may be gained through increased corporate focus, allowing management to concentrate their efforts on the core business of the "new" company.

Evidence suggests a wide range of results when it comes to divestitures and value creation, and not all diversified companies should be subjected to a "conglomerate" discount. Spin-offs, for instance, are more prevalent in fragmented and emerging industries, whereas the opposite holds true for mature sectors like utilities and consumer staples. Our case study highlights the importance of the balance between reduced agency costs and increased strategic flexibility, on one side, and the potential loss of value stemming from potential dis-synergies, on the other.

Moreover, size seems to be an important factor when it comes to the success of the SpinCo as a stand-alone company. Research shows that small firms, measured as having a market capitalization below USD 100m, materially underperform in relation to larger spun-out companies. See Bülow and Mjörnemark (2019).

Letting go is never easy, but nevertheless, this chapter concludes that management and boards should be strongly incentivized to develop a thorough portfolio allocation process in order to continuously re-evaluate the business portfolio.

We end this chapter by listing a few bullet points that can assist management in identifying opportunities where untapped potential may be released by an asset sale or a spin-off.

Underperforming stock and/or conglomerate discount

- The stock trades with a sum-of-parts discount and is undervalued relative to "intrinsic" value. Would part of the business be worth more to a different set of investors or owners?
- Parent company and business unit have different "investor stories" when it comes to exposure to factors like growth, yield, and risk.

Capital allocation and financial targets

- Does the company have a clear "market-based" capital allocation model in place? For example, do the different business units have separately stated financial targets, cost of capital, and incentive structures, or are policies dictated by the core business alone?

- Does the company have sufficient management capabilities to grow and develop all the businesses in its portfolio?

Best owner—the strategic and operational perspective

- A specific business unit might not fit the strategic direction the parent company is aiming for. Does the parent company have its competitive advantages in production excellence, like many industrial companies have, or in marketing and branding skills like branded consumer goods companies? Or its strength might emanate from its R&D capabilities rather than from a strong sales and distribution reach. These are examples of factors that strongly influence whether a breakup would allow for a more tailored operating business model.
- Is a business unit's performance lagging behind that of its peers? Or are a business units' cost structures not in line with peers?
- Are the incentive structure or the strategic flexibility limiting factors?

Lost synergies from a demerger

- What will a de-merger price tag look like in terms of lost synergies such as higher SG&A and procurement costs?
- Is the proposed SpinCo big enough to be on its own? Is the core business model strong enough? If not, a trade-sale could make more sense.

Public or private owner

- Being outside the public capital markets can for some companies bring relative advantages when it comes to factors like financial leverage, management incentives, and corporate governance policies.

References

BCG (2016) Creating Value Through Active Portfolio Management—The 2016 Value Creators Report.

Bülow S, Mjörnemark NG (2019) The Spinoff Scorecard: An Investment Strategy to Separate the Best Performing Spinoffs from the Worst. Copenhagen Business School.

EY (2019) Will You Set the Divestment Pace, or Try to Keep Up with It? Global Corporate Divestment Study.

Lee DD, Madhavan R (2010) Divestiture and Firm Performance: A Meta-Analysis. Journal of Management 36(6): 1345–1371.

Leimann C (2009) Værdiskabelse gennem frasalg og spaltning: Analyse af Danisco A/S og Novo Nordisk A/S. Institut for Okonomi Arhus Universitet.

Schulman L (2017) How Premium Conglomerates Sustain Success. Published Online. https://www.bcg.com/publications/2017/corporate-strategy-value-creation-premium-conglomerates-sustain-success.

Tjärnström H (2014) Unibet to Propose Distribution of Kambi. Published Online. https://www.kindredgroup.com/media/press-releases/2014/Unibet-to-propose-distribution-of-kambi/.

CHAPTER 7

Shareholder Remunerations—Time to Give Back?

Given some of the findings presented so far in this book, it should not come as a surprise that the equity market in many cases has a very strong focus on management returning excessive cash to shareholders. One of the most common capital allocation mistakes is no doubt when corporates with a strong free cash flow, a low debt level, and presence in mature markets try to achieve growth at too high a price.

As such, decisions regarding pay-out policies are closely tied to the balance sheet. But capital structure and financial leverage set aside, there are other considerations to take into account when it comes to shareholder distribution activity. One is to ask how large a part of the earnings a company can afford to pay out given it wants to stay competitive in the business in the long run. Or as the red queen in Alice in Wonderland puts it, how much running does it take, to keep in the same place (hint: start by taking a look at the ROIC level). For companies with a negative ROIC versus WACC-spread and/or a price book that trades below 1x, the burden of proof for retaining earnings in the business rests heavily with the management team. In this kind of companies, a retained dollar

T. Arenbo, *Capital Allocation and Value Creation*,
https://doi.org/10.1007/978-3-031-47048-6_7

will most likely be worth less to the shareholders than a dollar given out in dividends.[1]

The same line of reasoning can be applied to retaining earnings for growth purposes. The value of any incremental investment should over time meet or exceed the relevant cost of capital required. The most challenging part in this exercise is obviously to estimate the expected future returns on investments. However, as the chapter on divestitures demonstrated, there is another layer of complexity that is particularly evident in companies with multiple divisions exhibiting varying profitability levels. There is a potential risk that strong cash flows generated by the core business are reinvested in underperforming non-core ventures, instead of being returned to shareholders.

Why Dividend Policy Matters for Value Creation

From a purely theoretical perspective, pay-outs to shareholders do not create any value for shareholders because they do not increase the cash flow from the firm.

Even so, research on changes in dividend policies and their impact on shareholder value has indicated a positive relationship between increasing the distribution policy and generating short-term excess returns. Additionally, companies with higher dividend yields tend to have less volatile stock prices.

There are several reasons why this can be the case. For instance, a company that consistently increases its dividend pay-out over time signals to the market that it has confidence in its financial position and future earnings prospects.

Moreover, companies that pay out higher dividends tend to attract and retain investors who value a high dividend yield on their investments. These investors may be less likely to sell their shares during times of market volatility, which can help stabilize the company's stock price.

[1] The "one dollar test" involves examining whether a company or product can generate more than one dollar of profit for every dollar invested or spent. The idea behind the "one dollar test" is to ensure that a business can generate a positive return on investment (ROI) and be financially viable. If a company or product cannot generate at least one dollar of profit for every dollar invested, it may indicate that the business model is not profitable or that the product is not economically viable.

Last but not least, companies that pay out higher dividends may be seen as more disciplined in their capital allocation decisions. The empirical findings once again support the arguments made earlier in this book regarding the risks associated with cash usage directed towards CEOs who may have overly ambitious growth goals that may result in low returns for shareholders. Thus, in this case, increased dividends can mitigate some of the so-called principal-agent problem.

The Power of Compounded Dividends

"Yield" as an investment strategy might not have been the most popular strategy among investors in recent times, but our TSR study presented in Chapter 3, confirms how important a role a disciplined capital allocation process plays for long-term returns. This is partly due to the compounding effects of reinvested dividends.

Reinvesting dividends can be one of the least risky ways to grow wealth over the long term, as it allows the investment to grow exponentially over time. In markets with more mature industries, the need to reinvest for future growth is less important. As a result, the pay-out ratios are higher and the proportion of returns coming from dividends can be greater than that from price appreciation. Although the US equity market measured in price terms has significantly outperformed Europe since the financial crisis, the gap begins to close when we look at total shareholder returns. Dividends have over the past 20 years accounted for approximately one-third of the total return of the S&P500. In Europe, where the proportion of returns coming from dividends is typically higher than in the United States, dividends have over the same period contributed to around 45% of the total return.

Among our Nordic companies in the top-performing quartiles, we find several examples where the proportion of the return coming from dividends is around 50%. That is, for instance, the case for Swedish Match, Elisa, Axfood and Orion. Moreover, as indicated earlier in this chapter, companies with high dividends tend to display a lower share price volatility.

Ways to Distribute Excess Cash

If a company decides to let go of retained earnings, there are a few options to choose among. The most common way to distribute excess cash to shareholders is through **ordinary dividends**. It is a regular payment made to shareholders in proportion to the number of shares they hold. The amount and frequency of dividends are decided by the company's board of directors.

A second option is to pay out an **extra dividend**. This is a one-time payment made to shareholders in addition to regular dividends. This is often done when a company has a particularly large amount of excess cash.

A **share redemption programme** allows shareholders to sell back their shares to the company in exchange for cash. The company then retires these shares, reducing the total number of outstanding shares.

A **share buyback programme** is when a company buys its own shares from the market, reducing the number of outstanding shares and increasing the value of remaining shares. In theory, this should be a preferred mean of distribution when a company believes that its shares are undervalued in relation to its so-called intrinsic value.

Each of these options has its own advantages and disadvantages, and the company must carefully consider its goals, financial position, and market conditions before choosing the best option for distributing excess cash.

Ordinary Dividends

When it comes to dividends and the policy attached to them, effective communication with investors is critical. It is essential to ensure that dividend policies are clear, consistent, and rational. Any uncertainty in the company's dividend policy can confuse investors and potentially drive them away. Furthermore, decisions regarding dividend policy should, as mentioned earlier, be based on the company's growth prospects, reinvestment requirements, and overall capital allocation strategy.

When deciding to pay dividends, companies need to understand the potential impact on their valuation, as it can attract or repel investors based on their investment preferences. Companies that pay consistent and growing dividends are often viewed positively by investors, as these companies are perceived as financially stable and committed to sharing their profits with shareholders.

Once a company announces its intention to initiate or increase a regular dividend, the market tends to view it as a permanent commitment. As a result, any changes in the dividend policy can be interpreted by the market as a signal of the company's future prospects of cash flow generation or a change in the capital allocation priorities.

Share Buybacks (SBB)

Share buybacks have been a popular way to distribute means to shareholders in the United States, with companies spending trillions of dollars on buybacks over the past few decades. However, the practice has not been as common in Europe, where companies tend to prefer paying out dividends instead. This is partly due to cultural and regulatory differences, with European investors valuing stability and dividend income more highly than American investors. Additionally, some European countries have stricter rules around buybacks, requiring companies to have a minimum level of reserves before they can repurchase shares. According to a study by Goldman Sachs (2019), US companies spent around 25% of their cash usage on share buybacks between 2010 and 2019, while European companies spent just 5% over the same period.

The Buffet approach to share buybacks adds a new level of expertise required for a corporate capital allocator. At Berkshire Hathaway, share buybacks are not merely a method of returning surplus cash to shareholders, but a potential investment opportunity. However, in order to qualify as prioritized cash deployment usage, the stock should, with some margin, be valued below its intrinsic value. That means corporate management has to be able to distinguish between price and value. Only the most skilled corporate managers have the confidence to adopt this seldom deployed approach to capital allocation. However, CEOs who actually do possess the skill of telling price apart from value can prove to be a true blessing for the continuing shareholders of a company, a point that was made very evident in Thorndike's book "Outsiders".

SBB—What to Consider?

One of the main risks associated with share buybacks is the cyclical pattern they often follow. Companies tend to buy back shares when their stock is expensive which poses a big risk to the potential "return" the share buybacks will yield.

Another factor to consider is the company's need for financial flexibility. For instance, companies that are in a mature stage in their life-cycle may be better suited for dividends than share buybacks. In contrast, companies that are still growing and investing in their business may opt for share buybacks instead of paying dividends due to the higher degree of flexibility a SBB programme offers.

Furthermore, it is important to ensure that share buybacks are not hindering the ability to increase dividends. Shareholders may prefer to receive regular dividend payments rather than the potential benefits of share buybacks. Lastly, companies should consider the tax implications of share buybacks versus dividends. Share buybacks may be taxed differently than dividends, which can affect the tax liability of both the company and its shareholders.

Conclusions

For many companies, the dividend policy is an important tool for forming a long-term stable shareholder base, and as such, the policy should be as consistent and persistent as possible. Thus, the shareholder distributions should reflect both the *long-term free cash flow expectations* and the *marginal returns on investments*. Again, management should be held accountable for ensuring that the return on retained earnings meets its alternative uses, whether it be through dividends, share buybacks, or debt amortization.

Managers must be aware of how the market typically views the predictability of dividends and how it may react to any reduction thereof. A good way to determine the level of ordinary dividends is to stress-test future cash flows and choose a level that can be delivered with some certainty. After all, dividends for many companies are the residual of the conservatively estimated cash flow minus other value-creating alternatives.

Our next chapter will show how the dividend policy can be linked to decisions surrounding what might constitute an "optimal" capital structure.

Reference

Goldman Sachs (2019) Buyback Realities. Published Online. https://www.goldmansachs.com/insights/pages/top-of-mind/buyback-realities/report.pdf

CHAPTER 8

The Balancing Act of Finding the "Optimal" Capital Structure

Now we turn our attention from the asset side to the liability side of the balance sheet and analyze the role of capital structure in the value creation process. How much leverage can the business model take and how large, if any, are the financial gains from increasing the leverage?

Given the low interest rates of recent decades, there has been a strong case for a higher leverage, for example, through an equity-to-debt strategy that after the global financial crises became common in the United States. However, with increased leverage comes increased financial risks. And the risks can come in many shapes: new share issues at low valuations with risk of large ownership dilutions, weak balance sheets that can force companies to divest assets at discounted prices, and access to funding that can dry up as debt investors head for safe havens. Just to mention some examples of financial distress costs, we have seen recently. Thus, it is key to find the right balance between business and financial risk!

T. Arenbo, *Capital Allocation and Value Creation*,
https://doi.org/10.1007/978-3-031-47048-6_8

Capital Structure from the Academic Perspective

Since the formulation of the Miller and Modigliani propositions over 60 years ago, financial economists have been debating whether there is such a thing as an optimal capital structure—a proportion of debt to equity that can be expected to maximize long-run shareholder value.

A good start to this discussion is to briefly refresh our earlier discussions about the cost of capital. According to the theory about WACC, the beta of a stock increases if leverage goes up. In real life, the perception of risk is less dynamic, making the cost of equity less sensitive to incremental changes in leverage—at least up to a certain point, at which the equity market starts to get nervous and reprice the risk accordingly.

The opportunity for using leverage as a value-creating tool differs between companies and sectors. Companies with high EV/EBITDA multiples will typically see their leverage be constrained by the Debt/EBITDA ratio; thus, impact of leverage on overall valuation will be smaller. However, companies that can maintain debt levels between 20 and 40% of enterprise value can meaningfully reduce their cost of capital, as seen in sectors such as utilities and telecom.

And this is precisely what Private Equity funds have mastered so skillfully. One study, see L'Her (2016), shows that PE funds on average increase leverage almost three-fold compared to listed companies, from around 20% of EV to 60%. The same study also claims that PE funds' success to a relatively large degree can be explained by this higher leverage.

For the right company with the right owners, capital costs can thus be saved by increasing the share of debt funding. However, when setting the capital structure, specific factors must be considered, such as the **cost of financial distress** and the **"option value" of financial flexibility**. Before examining our preferred method of analyzing the capital structure, we will begin with a brief review of what the textbook says on this topic. See Barclay and Smith (2020).

Minimizing the Cost of Capital

The traditional theory of capital structure states that when the weighted average cost of capital (WACC) is minimized, the optimal capital structure is reached.

The optimal capital structure is affected by taxes, bankruptcy costs, agency costs, and asymmetric information and market inefficiencies. Without these "flaws", Modigliani and Miller stated, the value of a firm is unaffected by its capital structure and solely decided by the asset side of the balance sheet. There is, in other words, no magic leverage to use as guidance to achieve real-world optimal capital structure. But here are a few ways to think about it.

The Pecking Order and the Signalling Theory

In practice, the pecking order and the signalling theory need to be taken into consideration. The pecking order theory and the signalling theory are related in that they both consider the effects of asymmetrical information in financing decisions.

The pecking order theory takes a very different approach compared to the classic WACC model. Instead, it suggests that when a company wants to raise finance, it does so in the following pecking order: first is retained earnings, then debt, and finally equity as a last resort.

The signalling theory states that when companies make investment decisions, they also communicate information about their financial health to the market. This communication, or signal, can have a significant impact on the perceived value of the company and its ability to raise finance.

Debt as a Corporate Governance Tool

If you have read this far in the book, it should come as no surprise that debt can act as a very efficient corporate governance tool, especially for cash rich companies longing for growth.

The agency costs of the free cash flow hypothesis proposed by Jensen (1986) argues that when managers have more cash than is needed to fund all positive NPV projects (i.e. the free cash flow), there is a risk that managers will use the excess cash on unprofitable growth activities.

A firm's owners may decide to use a relatively large amount of debt to constrain the managers. A high debt ratio raises the threat of bankruptcy, which forces managers to be more careful with shareholders' money.

Capital Structure from a Practical Perspective

As a complement to the classical textbook models regarding capital structure, we would like to add a more practical dimension. When we discuss leverage with companies, they tend to place the focus on two factors: the risk of getting into **financial distress** and having sufficient **financial flexibility**.

The Cost of Financial Distress

For some companies, incurring too much debt can be very costly. We refer to these costs as "financial distress" costs, which can consist of:

Valuation Risks

A Harvard Business Review (2003) study concludes that companies with a predominance of intangible assets are most vulnerable to financial distress. In times of financial distress, knowledge-based industries, such as pharmaceutical, software, and communication equipment companies, face a risk of losing up to 80% of their enterprise value. In contrast, companies with mostly tangible assets, like those in agriculture, forest products, and real estate, typically experience much lower losses, averaging around 10%. The difference in risk between these two groups can be attributed to the challenges involved in evaluating them.

Knowledge-based industries heavily rely on intangible assets, such as research projects, intellectual property, and technological innovations. These assets are often complex and challenging for external parties, such as investors or creditors, to assess accurately. Their value is not immediately visible, and their future potential may be uncertain. As a result, during times of financial distress, when confidence in a company's ability to recover is low, investors tend to devalue or overlook these intangible assets, leading to substantial drops in enterprise value.

On the other hand, sectors like agriculture, forest products, and real estate have more tangible assets that are easier to appraise. Physical properties, equipment, and land can be readily valued, making it easier for external parties to understand and evaluate their worth. Consequently, when financial difficulties arise, the losses in these sectors are more limited, as tangible assets can act as a safety net and retain more of their value in the eyes of investors and stakeholders.

Sectors situated between these extremes include, for example, media, branded consumer products, and retailing.

Losing Business

Another potential cost of financial distress is related to the risk of losing business. If companies in some sectors are perceived as being financially vulnerable, clients may refrain from entering into long-term business agreements.

Ownership Dilution

If a company needs to do a share issue in the midst of a downturn or a financial crises, the potential dilution cost for the current owners can be very high.

Forced Divestments

Forced divestments are another potentially high cost of financial distress. Solvency and liquidity problems have forced many companies into unfavourable divestments in past economic downturns.

Underinvestment

When it comes to the various forms of financial distress costs, too high focus on cost-cutting measures must be factored into the equation. Our Lindab case study in Chapter 11 sheds some light on the hidden costs of too weak a capital structure in this perspective. These costs can, for example, include underinvestment as well as soft factors like negative cultural effects stemming from prolonged cost-cutting measures.

The potential costs of financial distress may to various degrees bring the "optimal" leverage down relative to what a "real-life" cost of capital-curve may suggest.[1] But there is more to it!

Option Value of Financial Flexibility

The liability side of the balance sheet can for some companies potentially contribute to value creation through what we could call the "option value" of financial flexibility. By that, we mean the potential value of being

[1] The shape of the theoretical WACC curve is to a large extent a reflection of the dynamics of the credit risk stemming from the risk of default and loss given a default.

able to act opportunistically "through the cycle" when it comes to factors like:

Strategic Capex
Companies may be able to add value by having the ability to increase, or at least pursue planned strategic investments in a downturn. But the "option value" may also include maintained or even increased spending on R&D, marketing, and capex when competitors might be cutting down on expenses. (More on this topic in Chapter 11.)

Acquisitions
The same reasoning can be applied to acquisitions as well, where a higher financial flexibility allows a company to act fast and opportunistically at potentially depressed valuations. It could also, as a complement to a strong balance sheet, be cost efficient to have covered funding commitments in place in order to minimize the need for new commitments during financially challenging times.

Companies with a strong growth strategy have a lot to lose if the balance sheet becomes too leveraged and the equity market starts to question the growth story from a funding perspective. That is why most companies with strong growth prospects, like NIBE and Assa Abloy, have chosen a very strong capital structure base to build upon.

Dividends Through the Cycle
Companies that can maintain a stable dividend through the cycle may mitigate the worst share price pressures as the dividend yield can act as a downside protection.

Working Capital and Customer Finance
There may be a strategic value in being able to loosen payment terms for customers and suppliers in periods of liquidity constraints. During the aftermath of the pandemic and ensuing supply-side distortions, we have for example seen a great value of keeping a high level of inventory.

How to Measure Leverage

Now we have a way to think about and analyze the topic of an "optimal" capital structure. But how can we measure it?

There are several options for measuring leverage, including price to book, interest rate coverage, debt to EBITDA, debt to enterprise value, and free cash flow to debt, which are some of the more commonly used methods. The **price to book ratio** could be hard to interpret as the book value of assets tells you very little about their true value. The second one, **EBIT or EBITDA interest coverage** is sometimes used as a covenant in bank lending. However, if interest rates are low, it is rarely a suitable ratio for deciding upon an appropriate capital structure. Therefore, for most sectors, we recommend to be careful when using any of these two ratios.

The lending market is, as we mentioned earlier, very focused on the **debt to EBITDA** ratio. The popularity probably stems from the measure being a crude proxy for a company's cash flow generation. But it disregards the reinvestment needs and thus may overestimate what is left to pay down debt for a company on an ongoing basis. A mistake often seen is that lenders use debt/EBITDA ratios to compare borrowing capacity among companies in different sectors, without adjusting for the capex intensity of that industry. For publicly listed companies, it is rather unusual to see debt/EBITDA ratios above 3x, except for companies in sectors like telecom, utility, and real estate.

The equity market typically uses debt to EBITDA in combination with **debt to enterprise value**. The latter ratio provides an implicit adjustment for the limitations of the Debt to EBITDA ratio, as different sectors are valued based on varying Enterprise Value to EBITDA multiples, partially due to the varying reinvestment requirements. If debt to EV reaches levels around 40% and if cash flow prospects at the same time are deemed as insecure, the equity market often starts worrying about the leverage and might, as a consequence, also start to discount a new share issue.

A relatively infrequently used measure is the **Free Cash Flow to Debt ratio**. When normalized levels of investments are considered, it indicates the length of time it would take a company to repay its debt. This measure is used by rating agencies like Moody's and Standard & Poor's but not so much by the equity market. Hopefully, all of the last three measures are aligned, but if they are not, leverage should in many cases be constrained by the weakest of the numbers.

Rating Agencies and Capital Structure

To illustrate how the more advanced part of the debt market thinks about credit quality and leverage, we will conduct a brief review of how the leading rating agencies, Standard & Poor's, Moody's, and Fitch, approach the topic. But before that, it may be helpful to place corporate credit ratings in a historical context. After the global financial crisis, the rating agencies faced a lot of criticism for their participation in the subprime market. And rightfully so. However, their major failure was due to the way they rated structured products like CDOs and CLOs. Their corporate methodology, which we are concerned with, held up well, and the historical data on defaults showed a high correlation with their rating assessment over a longer time period. The harsh criticism of their quantitative rating models prompted the agencies to become much more transparent in their corporate rating models. Hence, a lot of information on the subject is available and a very brief summary of the basics is provided below.

The target group for the global rating companies is primarily geared towards larger firms. For smaller firms, there are other rating agencies that are more appropriate. The underlying principles of the different agencies, however, remain the same. The initial step in assessing credit risk is to divide the analysis into two basic risk parameters: business risk and financial risk. These two parameters are either combined into a business and financial risk matrix (as used by Standard & Poor's) or into a weighted scorecard model (as used by Moody's).

The breakdown of Standard & Poor's **business risk profile** includes credit-driving factors such as the industry structure and the firm's competitive position within that sector. The industry structure is further broken down into factors such as cyclicality, growth trends, and competitive environment. The firm's competitive position, in turn, revolves around competitive advantages, scale, profitability, and operating efficiency. Standard & Poor's complements the qualitative assessment of the business risk with a quantitative approach based on the EBITDA margin level and its volatility. This approach shows the same information as the margin volatility ratio that we use as a factor when evaluating the cost of capital. As mentioned in Chapter 4 about earnings quality, there is a clear connection between a rating agency's business risk assessment and the (unlevered) cost of equity of a company. After all, it is the same cash flow that pays both debt holders and equity holders.

The **financial risk profile** is assessed by focusing on cash flow based measures. Key credit measures like Net debt/EBITDA and funds from operations/net debt are used in combination with a cash flow forecast for the company. Before a final rating evaluation is made, additional considerations such as the firm's financial targets and corporate governance policies, are taken into account. Companies that have, or aim to acquire, a rating are forced to think about their "debt story" in a structured way. Especially so in relation to the "equity story" and the shareholder value proposal, but also in relation to the funding risks. This process of structurally thinking about the capital structure from an equity perspective can in itself be of great value.

Conclusion

Capital structure considerations are tightly tied to the capital allocation and value creation prospects. But it is also tied to the equity markets and what they perceive as being an appropriate balance sheet. However, as we have stated earlier, the equity markets' perception can be "digital" in nature with rapid changes between having appropriate leverage versus becoming too highly indebted. The actual leverage levels seen in the market place suggest that finding the optimal capital structure in real life is about much more than just minimizing the short to medium-term WACC.

The academic world has long been puzzled by the inconsistent and sometimes opposing conclusions drawn from different theories on capital structure. Some academics support Miller and Modigliani's view that capital structure is of limited importance, as it has only a limited, predictable impact on corporate financing. On the other hand, others believe that corporate financing decisions reflect a balancing act between the tax benefits of increased debt and the higher risk of financial distress. However, if too much debt can harm a company's value, Jensen and others have shown that, for companies in stable, low-growth industries, too little debt can result in overinvestment and lower returns on capital.

For most companies, we believe, the potential costs of excessive leverage outweigh the costs of underleveraging. Given that economic and financial tail risks cannot be precisely anticipated in likelihood and magnitude, any leverage should in most cases err on the side of caution. For instance, companies with a positive ROIC spread and reasonable growth prospects should focus on managing the capital structure for **financial**

flexibility, which includes keeping leverage relatively low. This group should aim to maintain a flexible capital structure that provides room for manoeuvring and helps them take advantage of growth opportunities as they arise.

On the other hand, for companies with a lower and more volatile ROIC, the decision regarding capital structure should be heavily influenced by the risk and potential cost of **financial distress**. For such companies, the mismanagement of the liability side of the balance sheet can lead to severe value destruction. Thus, it is essential to focus on maintaining a sound capital structure that can withstand potential stress scenarios.

However, for a third group of companies, those with stable ROIC and low-growth prospects, the capital structure becomes a more evident tool for value creation. These companies, typically found in sectors such as telecom and real estate, can benefit from leverage as it not only reduces the cost of capital but also helps prevent management from overinvesting in low-growth markets.

In practice, many corporates set their capital structure targets based on "accepted wisdom" and peer comparisons. A more tangible way, and a help to increase owners and managers intuition about the capital structure, is to consider the following list of questions when deciding on an appropriate leverage target.

Potential financial gain of leverage

- Interest rates and corporate tax shield
  Does the interest rate and tax rate allow for a meaningful reduction in the cost of capital? Think in terms of Debt to Enterprise Value.
- Agency costs (debt as a corporate governance tool)
  Are the agency costs and risks of overinvestments high?

Benefits of funding flexibility

- Opportunities of "through the cycle" cash flow deployment
  How valuable is it to be able to maintain investments, acquisitions, R&D, and dividends through the cycle?

Risk of getting into financial distress

- Profitability and Cash flow volatility
  How high is the operational leverage?
- Need for external funds?
  Does the company need external funding in order to achieve its growth plans?
- Financial covenants
  Does the lending documentation contain covenants that may be breached?

Costs of financial distress

- Do customers care about bankruptcy risks?
  Is client relationship long term with an expected service and maintenance content?
- Investment need
  Sector and competitive perspective—can the company keep up with competitors even in a downturn?
- Assets can easily be valued by the market (or used as debt collateral)
  Are assets of a general character and easy to assess a value?
- The level of asymmetric information
  Is the information used to value the company of a transparent character?

Financial market and owner aspects of leverage

- Current owners' ability and willingness to contribute with more equity capital
  Do the current owners have the willingness and ability to contribute with more capital if need be?
- Risk preferences of owners and management
  Are owners and management worried or concerned about financial distress?
- Access to funding in different market conditions
  Market pricing of the stock under distressed circumstances? Does the company have a public rating?

References

Barclay MJ, Smith C (2020) The Capital Structure Puzzle: Another Look at the Evidence. Journal of Applied Corporate Finance 32(1): 80–91.

Harvard Business Review (2003) How Much Cash Does Your Company Need? Published Online. https://hbr.org/2003/11/how-much-cash-does-your-company-need

Jensen M (1986) Agency Costs of Free Cash Flow; Corporate Finance and Takeovers. American Economic Review 76(2): 323–339.

L'Her, JF, Stoyanova R, Shaw K, Scott W & Lai C (2016) A Bottom-Up Approach to the Risk-Adjusted Performance of the Buyout Fund Market. Financial Analysts Journal 72(4):1–13.

CHAPTER 9

Winning Financial Strategies—Funding and Risk Considerations

Based on the inherent characteristics of the business model, the desired risk level for the capital structure can be set. And based on the combined risk of the two, a funding and hedging policy can be developed. A higher risk level in the two first parts can be mitigated by a more conservative stance towards the latter part. We could call it "financial insurance". How to play the game depends partly on risk preferences and partly on the potential gains from taking on and paying for "insurance" (See Fig. 9.1).

Connecting and balancing the risk regarding the business model, capital structure and funding can be hard to do in practice. The first two parts in the process are often fairly well aligned. The boards, CEOs, and CFOs often have reasonably good understanding of balancing the risk between the business model and the capital structure—at least in the long run. However, when it comes to the third part, which to a larger extent is governed by the treasury department, excessive focus may be put on price rather than content, i.e. the "funding and risk insurance".

This chapter intends to give a brief overview of how to build a more robust funding position. We will start by reviewing the concept of "funding insurance" and describe different ways it could be attained.

T. Arenbo, *Capital Allocation and Value Creation*,
https://doi.org/10.1007/978-3-031-47048-6_9

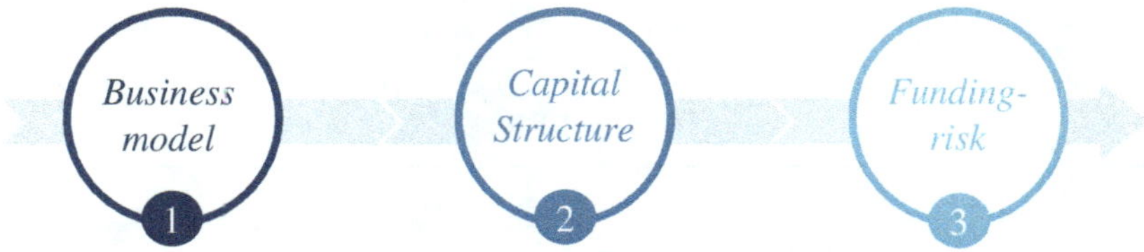

Fig. 9.1 Strike the desired balance and level of risk

Liquidity Back-up

The most important tool in the funding insurance toolbox is typically the liquidity back-up. The liquidity back-up can constitute cash on the balance sheet as well as off-balance sheet solutions. A bank that offers a revolving credit facility (RCF) is an example of an off-balance sheet liquidity. Excess cash on the balance sheet, i.e. cash in excess of what is needed from an operational perspective, is an example of on-balance liquidity back-up. The on-balance sheet liquidity back-up is funded by debt if the company has a net debt position; if not, the cash position is funded by equity. There is a considerable difference in the cost of the three various liquidity back-up solutions, where an off-balance sheet banking solutions are the cheapest, and the equity funded on-balance sheet cash position is the most expensive.

We have studied almost 300 Nordic corporates and found that the median cash buffer has been remarkably stable at 5–7% of sales since 2000. It is also evident that, on average, companies do not seem to have been hoarding cash since the GFC.[1]

Calibrating the fundamental need for liquidity in terms of cash and unutilized committed credit facilities is a delicate task which requires taking multiple perspectives into account. Looking beyond the liquidity requirement to maintain day-to-day operations, an analysis usually starts out by looking at the defensive part of the liquidity buffer. This part should cover liquidity outflows that firms need to maintain over-the-cycle. CAPEX, R&D spending, debt maturities, dividends, etc. are all important factors in building up this minimum liquidity need. However, looking beyond this we find that corporates also usually find a value in

[1] It is however possible that Nordic corporates have raised their total available liquidity by increasing their undrawn committed credit facilities.

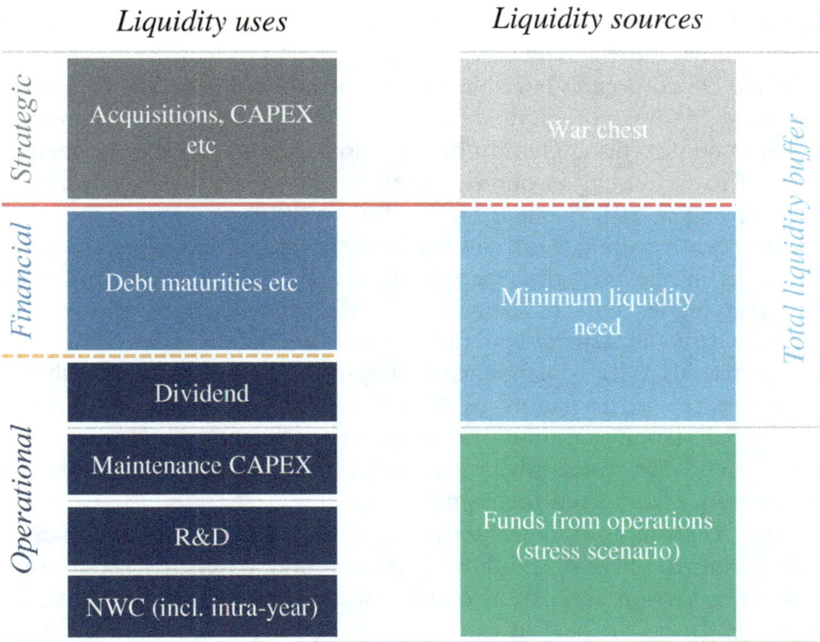

Fig. 9.2 A conceptual approach to calibrating the liquidity buffer

having liquidity in excess of that for more strategic and offensive purposes. For example, such a "war chest" creates financial flexibility to pre-fund growth CAPEX, acquisitions, and share buybacks or to use the balance sheet opportunistically during a downturn. For corporates with a business model highly dependent on their ability to make future acquisitions, the value of such a funding insurance can be very high. In some cases, this part of the liquidity position can, in fact, constitute the majority of the total buffer (Fig. 9.2).

Access to Capital

The global financial crisis highlighted the value of having a diversified pool of funding sources. While bank lending volumes contracted, capital market-based bond issuances actually went in the opposite direction during 2009. Thus, for those corporates having already established a presence in the bond or private placement markets prior to the crisis, this proved to be of great value.

While US corporates have been using the capital markets as their main source of funding for quite some time, Europe is now slowly moving in the same direction. The Nordics are no exception, where the median share of bank funding in our sample of Nordic corporates has decreased to some 75% in 2017 from as high as 90% in 2008.

A key driver behind this trend has been the tighter regulations imposed on banks in the post-crisis period (Basel III). The deleveraging pressure and higher cost of capital have effectively changed the role of banks, where the general appetite for an "originate and hold" strategy has decreased. With a dampened willingness to expand balance sheets, banks are now acting more as flexible liquidity providers in terms of committed standby facilities and shorter-term financings. One example is the trend for event-driven financings being bridged by banks for longer-term take-outs in the capital markets.

From a financial insurance perspective, the use of debt capital markets is not only to diversify funding sources. Bond covenants often come in a softer version compared to those seen in bank lending and access to longer tenors enables an extension (and potential smoothing) of the maturity profile. Furthermore, it can increase commitment headroom with banks for event-driven financings and limit the dependence on an overly large bank group.[2]

Credit Rating

The main value of a credit rating lies in its ability to increase access to capital and lower the cost of funding. Having a public rating generally provides increased funding flexibility during normal market conditions, including a wider range of available options for debt structure and maturity. It also grants rated corporates easier access to funding, compared to unrated issuers in more challenging market conditions, serving as a form

[2] Using bank financing for short-term execution of event-driven funding increases flexibility and keeps non-disclosure material to a limited group, i.e. during IPOs or M&As. Furthermore, it bridges any subsequent take-out in the bond market, which can then be properly timed and positioned.

of financial insurance. Additionally, a credit rating may improve the short-term loan market capacity as the prospects to "take out" loans in the debt capital markets improve.

However, there are some potential drawbacks associated with having a public rating. Firstly, publicly rated companies face increased scrutiny from investors, analysts, and regulators, which can restrict managerial discretion and impose additional reporting requirements. Secondly, public ratings expose a company's creditworthiness and financial position to competitors, suppliers, and customers, potentially impacting negotiating power and strategic relationships. Additionally, credit ratings are subjective assessments and may be biased and subject to conflicts of interest.

Maturity Profile

Liability management is important from a financial insurance perspective since a well spread maturity profile and a longer duration result in a lower share of yearly redemptions. As such, it can help to mitigate the exposure to cyclicality as well as to potential changes in the credit quality.

Looking at our Nordic sample, we do not see any clear signs that corporates have increased the duration of their debt in the post-crisis period. The average maturity has been relatively stable at around three years since 2007. On average, around 20–25% of the interest-bearing debt has been defined as short term over the same period. This stands in contrast to how corporates fund themselves in the United States, where the duration of the debt typically is much longer.

Hybrid Bonds

A hybrid bond is a subordinated instrument that combines debt and equity features within the corporate capital structure. These hybrid instruments have gained popularity due to their ability to diversify funding sources and provide a form of "funding insurance". One advantage of these quasi-equity instruments is their potential to enhance senior credit metrics, as viewed by both International Financial Reporting Standards (IFRS) and rating agencies. This improvement in credit metrics can have a positive impact on a company's creditworthiness and borrowing costs. Additionally, these instruments possess loss-absorbing features, which can be valuable in situations of financial distress or default, offering a layer of protection for investors and lenders.

However, there are potential drawbacks to consider. Firstly, the complexity of hybrid instruments can make them difficult to understand and assess. Secondly, the issuance and maintenance of these instruments may incur higher costs compared to traditional debt or equity. Lastly, the unique features of hybrid instruments may limit their appeal to certain types of investors, and their valuation can be challenging due to the lack of standardized methodologies. Additionally, regulatory considerations add complexity and may restrict the flexibility of issuers and investors. Careful evaluation and professional advice are important when considering the inclusion of hybrid instruments in the capital structure.

Key Credit Ratios and FX Risks

An often overlooked aspect of funding risk is the choice of currency composition for the debt. Determining the optimal currency split on debt depends on various priorities and strategies. Some companies aim to maximize net profit by minimizing tax payments and interest rate costs. Others focus on hedging book equity, while some prioritize minimizing volatility in the Net debt/EBITDA ratio. The choice of strategy depends on a company's affordability and the availability of currency funding options.

Conclusions—Putting the Pieces Together

The choice of capital structure will not only be a result of the factors mentioned in the previous chapters, but will also be an interaction with how the leverage is created. A high leverage can be combined with a lower level of funding risk, for example, through a long and diversified maturity profile and strong liquidity. This funding set-up, which is more common in the United States than in Europe, mitigates the risks of higher leverage.

If the treasury department focuses too heavily on "price" rather than "insurance content" of the funding and hedging products, this can result in an "underinvestment" in financial insurance. In order for the treasury to act optimally, it needs to see and understand the full picture of the value creation, from the business model and its equity story, through the choice of leverage to the actual choice of funding and hedging. How the board of directors chooses to set up the financial policy is crucial for a good downstream implementation. In Fig. 9.3, we list some companies that we regard as having (or have had) a financial set-up that in a good way links these pieces together.

Company	Business model	Capital structure	Funding	Outcome
Com Hem (prior to merger with Tele2)	• High share of recurring income • Fairly low cost of financial distress	• 35% debt/EV • Mid BB rating • Target leverage 3.5-4x	• Strong liquidity • Long and well diversified maturity profile • High funding diversification	➢ **Gains from high leverage heavily outweighed costs of funding insurance**
Assa Abloy	• Value adding growth (10%/year) model • Stable cash Flows • Low cost of Equity	• 10% debt/EV • A- rating • Target leverage<2x	• Diversified funding • Well spread maturities • No covenants • ALM match (FX)	➢ **Low leverage and low funding risk due to profitable growth opportunities**
Ericsson	• High R&D and high share of intangible assets • High cost of financial distress • High cost of Equity	• Net cash position of 0-10%/EV • BBB-/Ba1 • Target: Net cash (excl pension liabilities)	• Strong liquidity • Cash to sales >20% • Balance sheet cash funded primarily by long bonds	➢ **Low leverage and low funding risk due to high financial distress costs**

Fig. 9.3 Balanced risk between business model, capital structure, and funding

PART III

Reading the Market and Thinking Like an Investor

The market contains an abundance of information, which can be a valuable source of input for a firm's decisions regarding capital allocation and cash flow deployment. However, in order to effectively make use of the market information, corporate executives must possess the ability to interpret the market and extract relevant insights.

A good starting point is to have a fair understanding of the financial and macro-economic landscape. Therefore, the first chapter in this part aims to give a brief description of the current financial regime and what may lie ahead of us.

Academic research claims that the capital market is better at allocating capital efficiently than corporate managers. The conglomerate discount discussed in Chapter 6 further highlights the challenges a company faces around its internal capital market. In the second chapter of this part, we investigate how "thinking like an investor" can improve a firm's capital allocation process. We will specifically focus on three skills where investors typically excel: understanding the trade-off between risk and return, using scenario analysis and expected value, and having a disciplined and rule-based approach to investing. This chapter revolves to a large extent around what behavioural finance has taught us about cognitive biases and irrational behaviours that can impact our decision making.

The last chapter in this section is devoted to a recession study, where we investigate how these skills can be used in real life. We find that many of the factors explaining outperformance during a recession can be linked to the strategic flexibility of having a strong balance sheet. For many of the worst performers, the picture is reversed, with high indebtedness leading to an excessive focus on cost-cutting and debt reduction. Our study also highlights the importance for management to have a well-developed scenario planning in place, as well as a long-term perspective, in order to handle market and cash flow volatility.

CHAPTER 10

Financial and Macro-economic Backdrop

This book focuses on making effective capital allocation decisions, with financial market information being a crucial component of the decision-making process. However, the financial market's evaluation of a company's attributes, such as growth potential and margin stability, can vary over time and so can the availability of leverage as a value-generating tool. In this chapter, we take a step back in order to better understand how the investor preferences may change between various macro and financial policy regimes.

The intelligent investor is a realist who sells to optimists and buys from pessimists. Benjamin Graham

Pre-COVID-19—Great Moderation and Secular Stagnation

It is now 40 years since Thatcher and Reagan initiated the wave of deregulation of financial markets as well as global goods and services markets. In the so-called second wave of globalization, world trade has flourished and productivity increases were, at least initially, high. At the same time, we got independent central banks and a clear division in responsibilities between fiscal and monetary policy.

T. Arenbo, *Capital Allocation and Value Creation*,
https://doi.org/10.1007/978-3-031-47048-6_10

As a result of the strong supply-side forces combined with independent central banks with inflation mandates, inflation, and with it interest rates, fell sharply during the period. And in turn, lower (real and nominal) interest rates opened the way for higher corporate profits as well as equity valuations.

Not only have we seen the general asset appreciation outpacing the nominal GPD during the past couple of decades, but also the debt to GDP ratio has moved in the same direction. It is worth noting that the developed economies generally have not succeeded in amortizing debt levels after the debt crises like for example the GFC or various country-specific real estate related crisis. The only outcome from the debt induced crisis is that the growth rate of the debt build-up has temporarily slowed and that the debts have changed hands between the private and public sector.

If we zoom in on the period post the GFC, the compass needle steadily pointed towards what we have come to know as "secular stagnation"—a period characterized by low and stable inflation, low nominal and real interest rates, relatively low GDP growth, low volatility, and low-risk premiums on so-called safe assets.

Borio et al. (2017) summarized why the appearance of stability during the so-called secular stagnation period was so deceptive. They claim that during an extremely expansionary monetary policy, there have been imbalances that have mainly manifested themselves in the form of a strong build-up of debt, increased domestic inequalities, and large global trade imbalances.

The roots of many current imbalances can be traced back to an economy that is becoming increasingly liberalized and focused on supply. With monetary policy and inflation control being the primary stabilizing tools, politicians have neglected to address underlying imbalances and the need for economic reforms.

Over the past few decades, the traditional business cycle has been partially replaced by an asset price cycle (or financial cycle) as a result of monetary stabilization policies. However, there are costs associated with these policies, which primarily rely on credit growth to alleviate downturns. These costs include suboptimal market-based resource allocation and increased financial vulnerability due to excessive credit inflation.

It is no surprise that prior to the pandemic, markets viewed central bankers and their monetary policies as a guarantee for financial prices. The central bankers' impact on the financial markets had a significant effect on the risk premiums for not only the longer part of the yield curve, but also for riskier assets such as corporate bonds and stable-yielding equities (Fig. 10.1).

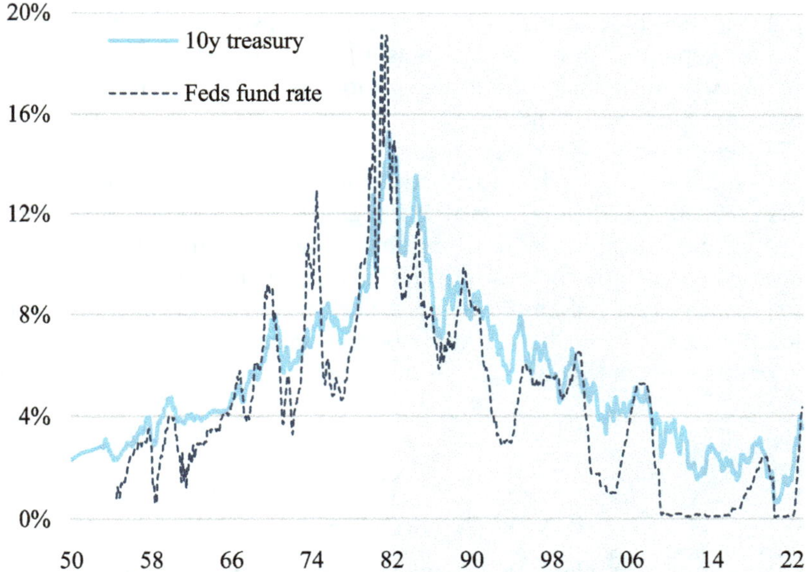

Keynesianism		**Neoliberalism**	
1. *Dependency ratio*	↗	1. *Dependency ratio*	↓
2. *Globalization*	→	2. *Globalization*	↑
3. *Productivity*	←	3. *Productivity*	↓
4. *Inequality*	↓	4. *Inequality*	↑
5. *Central Bank power*	→	5. *Central Bank power*	↑

Fig. 10.1 From Keynesianism to free markets and supply-side focus (*Source* http://www.econ.yale.edu/~shiller/data.htm)

The New Game Has Come—And We Are Still Making Up the Rules

Following the outbreak of the pandemic, policymakers in Europe and the United States face a new set of challenges. A strong fiscal response to the pandemic, combined with supply-side disruptions and a war, has let the inflation genie out of the bottle. It is worth noting that low and stable inflation was the primary driver behind low interest rates and the key to maintaining low-risk premiums.

There is now a greater awareness of the benefits of Keynesian policies, and politicians may be less eager to tighten fiscal policy in the coming years compared to their actions after the global financial crisis. A potential game-changer brought by fiscal dominance is that central banks will be pressured to support fiscal authorities through a stronger focus on yield curve control and full employment rather than solely on inflation. Ultimately, central bankers have a new world to adapt to, and so do financial markets as monetary policy is no longer a trusted put-option on financial prices.

Post-COVID-19—Are We Heading for a New "Financial Regime"?

The era of secular stagnation, as we knew it, was likely to give way to a new regime in due time anyway. The pandemic only acted as a catalyst for the extremely rapid change in monetary and financial regimes.

The macro and policy regime uncertainties, as well as their consequences for asset prices, are greater than we have seen in a very long time. We can envision several different scenarios for the future. At one end of the spectrum, we may see a "Japanification" of financial markets, characterized by very low inflation, higher real rates, and stock markets that show limited growth. At the other end of the spectrum, we may experience a reflationary setting with debt monetization or even stagflation, resulting in higher and more volatile inflation, higher risk premiums, and relatively low real rates. In this scenario, "real" assets are likely to perform well. However, if we can maintain a balance between these extremes, a continuation of the "Goldilocks" environment in financial markets may persist.

Given the relatively high probability of a debt monetization scenario, should we prepare ourselves for a world with "normalized" risk premiums, a world where central banks as the buyer of last resort no longer have unlimited power to suppress yield curves, term premiums, and credit spreads? This is a feasible scenario for various reasons. First, even if the inflation issue is resolved, the damage from a risk perspective has already been done to some extent. Investors, especially in the bond markets, have suffered losses and will likely require a larger safety margin for taking on long-term risks for many years to come. Secondly, the current inflation situation is more challenging for policy makers to navigate. In practice, this means a higher risk of policy mistakes and subsequent policy changes, which will also result in higher risk premiums for longer.

Financial Regimes and Valuation

In Fig. 10.2 where we visualize the correlation between real interest rates and equity valuation expressed in CAPE-terms,[1] it becomes very evident how different financial regimes bring different equity valuations. Since the GFC equity valuations have been considerably above the long-term averages which, at least to some extent, have been driven by low real rates and a stable inflation.[2]

Conclusions

The characteristics that drive a company's value can be given different weights by investors in various financial environments; and changes in financial market regimes may result in different approaches towards the three value drivers, leverage, and the overall risk level at which the company is operating.

And even though the market is a good indicator of intrinsic value in the long run, it occasionally fails dramatically. Or, as Warren Buffet puts it: "*Even though the business that the two of you own may have economic*

[1] CAPE is an abbreviation for cyclically adjusted price-to-earnings ratio and was invented by Robert Shiller in an attempt to better account for long-term trends in earnings and valuations.

[2] Low real rates are not the only reason why valuation multiples are at historically high levels. US/European tax reductions and higher expected long-term margins and ROIC add to that list. Moreover, in the United States, the compositions of the index has been more tilted towards highly valued tech companies.

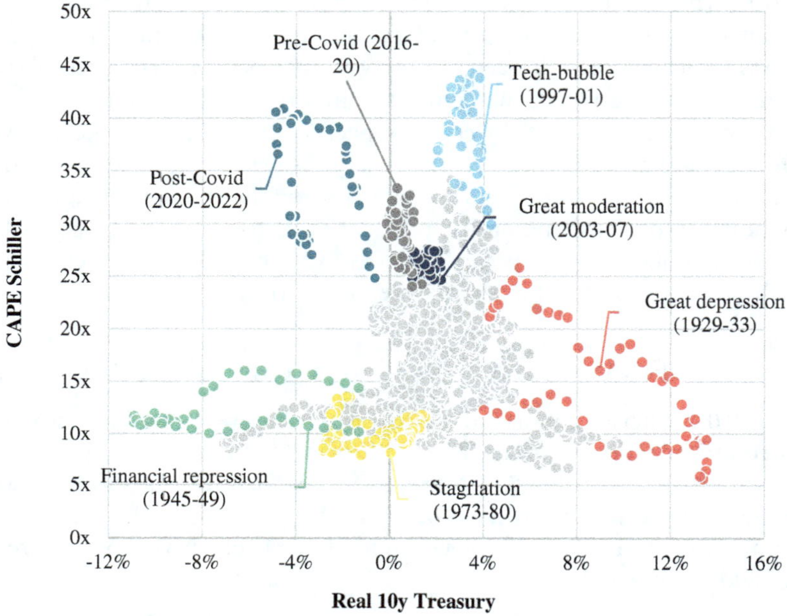

Fig. 10.2 CAPE ratio (*Source* http://www.econ.yale.edu/~shiller/data.htm)

characteristics that are stable, Mr. Market's quotations will be anything but. For, sad to say, the poor fellow has incurable emotional problems."[3]

When considering financial market regimes, equity valuation, and capital allocation decisions, we can think of several factors that need to be taken into account, with market sentiment and inflation related risk premiums being at the forefront.

- Coming back to Thorndike (2012), it turns out that seven out of the eight "outsiders" reviewed in his book had an acquisition strategy built on the virtue of being patient. The CEOs were return-oriented with a long-term perspective on value creation, which helped them staying on the side-lines during periods of elevated market pricing. On the other hand, they dared to be contrarian

[3] Buffet (1987).

when others were fearful, and making large and bold acquisitions at depressed valuations was an important ingredient in their success strategies.

- Not only is the attractiveness of making acquisitions influenced by the market sentiment, but so are the value-creating prospects of buying back your own shares. Figure 10.2 showed how strongly the pricing of a company's own currency, that is, the stock price, can be influenced by the prevailing financial regime. Thus, market sentiment and financial regimes can materially impact capital allocation decisions, such as those regarding SBBs or financing. For instance, the high stock market valuations observed post-COVID-19 saw many growth-oriented companies raise new equity on favourable terms.
- There is a significant likelihood that capital costs, especially for some sectors, will be higher in the future. With inflation re-emerging as a crucial factor, investors are now placing more value on pricing power and margin stability. Not all companies will be affected equally by rising risk premiums in this environment. For example, companies seeking market approval may need to re-evaluate the balance between investing for growth and maintaining margin resilience.
- The cost of debt relative to equity will change in an environment with higher and less predictable inflation. Some companies may have to reassess their leverage targets, access to funding, and liquidity. For certain asset classes, the "interest rate carry game" will become irrelevant. On a broader level, leverage as a tool for value creation may become less significant.
- Risk premiums can in a sense be viewed as the cost of "financial insurance" and may impact the way balance sheet risk and funding risk are considered. In a world where interest rate term premiums and credit spreads are elevated, reducing balance sheet risk may be a more cost-effective way to bring down overall financial risk than purchasing more expensive "funding insurance".

References

Borio C, Disyatat P, Juselius M, Rungcharoenkitkul P (2017) Why So Low for So Long? A Long-term View of Real Interest Rates. BIS Working Papers No. 685.

Buffet WE (1987) Letter to Shareholders, 1987 Berkshire Hathaway Annual Report.
Thorndike WN (2012) The Outsiders: Eight Unconventional CEOs and Their Radically Rational Blueprint for Success. Harvard Business School Publishing.

CHAPTER 11

Adopting an Investor Mind-Set

Part of the scope of this book is to improve the ability to read the market and make use of the information in the capital allocation process. Additionally, it aims to raise the awareness about the difference between the price and the value of an asset. And understanding financial markets and valuation is crucial for any outperforming investor. However, in this chapter, we will describe three additional investor skills which we believe could be of great benefit to corporate managers in their capital allocation process, namely:

- **Applying a disciplined rule-based framework for investing**
- **Thinking in terms of risk-reward trade-off**
- **Using various techniques for scenario modelling**

Effective capital allocation...requires a certain temperament. To be successful you have to think like an investor, dispassionately and probabilistically, with a certain coolness. Michael Mauboussin (Chapter 6 in Thorndike [2012])

T. Arenbo, *Capital Allocation and Value Creation*,
https://doi.org/10.1007/978-3-031-47048-6_11

Disciplined Rule-Based Investing

A crucial pillar in how to think like an investor is concerned with issues related to behavioural finance. The subject has received a lot of attention in the past few decades and has highlighted how individuals often deviate from rationality due to cognitive biases, emotions, and social factors. Common cognitive biases include loss aversion, overconfidence, and so-called anchoring, where individuals rely too heavily on initial information or reference points when making decisions.

Emotions like fear and greed can lead to irrational behaviour, such as excessive cost-cutting during a market downturn or poor supply-discipline during economic booms. In addition, social factors may play a role in behavioural finance. People tend to be influenced by the behaviour and opinions of others, which can contribute to market bubbles and crashes which, for instance, was the case during the period around the pandemic when the acronym FOMO (fear of missing out) well described part of the market sentiment.

Behavioural finance provides insights into the psychological biases and patterns of human behaviour that affect financial markets, investor behaviour, and overall economic outcomes. By recognizing these biases and patterns, executives can make more informed decisions and develop strategies to mitigate the negative effects of their own potentially irrational behaviour.

Professional investors try to mitigate these shortcomings by conducting disciplined, rule-based investing that involves following a set of guidelines or rules for making investment decisions. For an investor to be successful in the long run, there is, for example, no room to be stubborn. Investors need, at all times, to look for non-corroborating evidence and have trigger points to change their views. For instance, having predefined stop-losses or fall-back plans are typical "tools" investors work with.

In the context of a corporate executive and the capital allocation process, following a disciplined and rule-based approach that considers behavioural shortcomings can involve asking yourself questions like:

- Do we properly take into account the aspects of "competition neglect" and lack of "outside view" in our investment process?
- Do we avoid the temptation to chase overly ambitious growth targets without proper risk assessment?

- Where are the blind spots in relation to the base-case scenario?
- How do we respond to setbacks or underperforming investments? Are we prone to prematurely terminating projects due to short-term setbacks or holding on to failing investments for too long out of reluctance to take a potential loss?
- Do we maintain discipline and adhere to our capital allocation strategy even when faced with market volatility or pressure to pursue alternative options?

Again coming back to Thorndike (2012), embracing a rational and disciplined approach to resource allocation is a common feature among the eight CEOs and one of the main key takeaways from the book.

Develop a Risk vs. Reward Mind-Set

A second fundamental pillar in an investor's framework deals with the relation between risk and reward. And here it is important to emphasize that when we talk about risk, we refer to long-term economic risk to value creation, and not to stock price risk stemming from financial market volatility.

In real life, just like in investing, there are a lot of "rear-view mirror drivers" who fail to understand the basic concept of risk. Risk only exists "ex-ante", "ex-post" the outcomes are known to everyone. The concept of risk can be hard to understand. To start with it is subjective and different people have different risk tolerances based on for instance financial situation, investment goals, and not least, emotions.

People also often struggle with understanding probabilities and statistics, which are essential for evaluating risk. Instead, as we just reviewed, people tend to rely on heuristics (mental shortcuts) and emotions rather than objective data when making decisions. This topic was brought to a broader audience thanks to Kahneman (2012) and his book "Thinking, Fast and Slow" and well described by the author's quote:

> *We're blind to our blindness. We have very little idea of how little we know. We're not designed to know how little we know.*

However, the investor community is at least trying to mitigate these behavioural shortcomings by weighing expected returns against potential risks. Risk-adjusted returns provide a first basic step and more accurate way to compare investments that have different levels of risk. After all, investments with a higher potential return tend to come with higher risks, and vice versa.

Risk Tolerance

In developing an "investor way" of thinking about risk, a good start is to think about and in turn set an appropriate level for the "risk tolerance". This involves considering the extent of vulnerability and acceptable economic loss that the company and its owners can tolerate. The choice of risk level is to some extent tied to the questions about what constitutes a suitable capital structure. As such, it includes questions around the risk and costs associated with getting into financial distress. For instance, Chapter 12 will highlight how expensive it can be, in terms of ownership dilution, for those shareholders who lack the financial means to participate in a distressed share issuance. Additionally, our Nordic sample provides several examples of management and boards making large acquisitions without considering the risk preferences of the majority of shareholders. Some of the larger acquisitions made by companies like Ericsson, SSAB, and Telia resulted in considerable higher operational as well as financial risk, which was likely not something the majority of the class B shareholders were longing for.

Distribution and Probabilities

The next step in the process brings us to say a few words on risk and uncertainty, as the two concepts differ in an important aspect. Risk involves situations where the probabilities and potential outcomes can be assessed with some level of confidence. Uncertainty, on the other hand, refers to a situation where the distribution of outcomes is unknown or difficult to quantify. Unlike natural sciences, which typically deal with risks, social sciences unfortunately need to deal with uncertainties. Dealing with uncertainties makes decision-making more subjective and relies to a larger extent on judgement and scenario analysis.[1]

[1] Quantitative models can still be a useful tool for gaining a better understanding of sensitivities, even though a cautious approach needs to be taken towards the result they produce. A decision maker who intends to use quantitative models must, for example,

The normal distribution is widely used in finance and economics due to its simplicity and mathematical properties, such as its symmetrical shape. However, financial markets and economies often exhibit non-normal behaviour, such as fat-tailed or skewed distributions, heavy outliers, and volatility clustering. For example, credit default risk might be better modelled by a binomial distribution with binary outcomes. When accounting for the presence of outliers and heavy-tailed outcomes, the t-distribution is a commonly used option. Figure 11.1 depicts a stylized version of the probabilities of macro-economic scenarios with a skewed fat-tailed distribution.

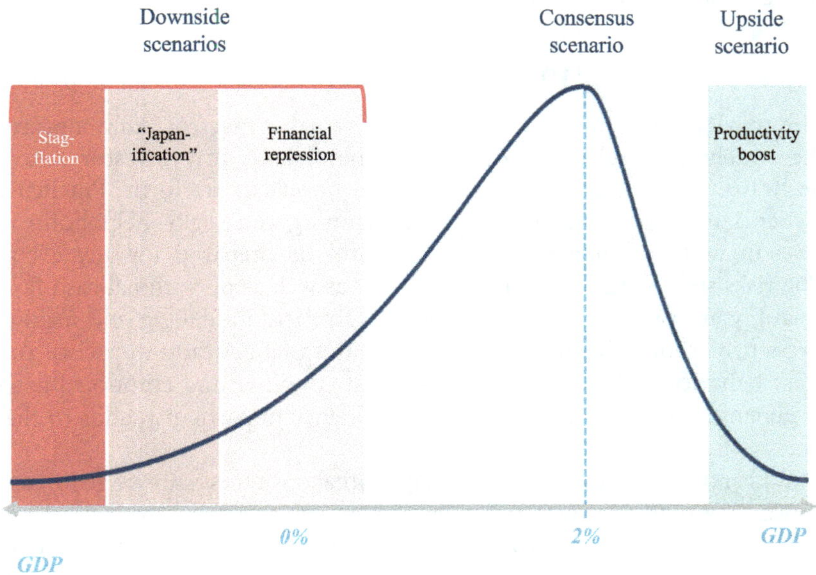

Fig. 11.1 A stylized version of the probabilities of potential macro-economic scenarios with a skewed fat-tailed distribution

be aware of what the underlying distribution governing the model looks like and the shortcomings it brings.

Expected Value

Once the probabilities of events are set, the expected value can be calculated. By using expected value[2] as a decision-making tool, the investment committee can quantify the potential outcomes and weigh them based on their likelihood of occurrence. This approach helps in prioritizing and selecting investments or a portfolio of projects that offer the highest expected value, while considering the associated risks.

However, it is worth noting that decision-making based on expected value is an iterative process. As new information becomes available or circumstances change, managers need to update the probabilities and reassess the expected values.

Thinking in Scenarios

The third and last pillar in our review of valuable investor skills concerns the widely used adoption of scenario modelling. Any investor knows by heart that predicting the future is an uncertain art form. Practicing scenario modelling and contingency planning can really help both an investor and a company to stay agile and be prepared for any event. The risks stemming from financial market as well as operational cash flow volatility are two important reasons why scenario modelling and making stress tests should be an integral part of a capital allocation process. But what behavioural finance teaches us about cognitive and emotional flaws in general, and some managers' overconfidence in particular, adds to that list.

Research shows that, when managers make forecasts about their cash flows, they tend to "over-extrapolate" past performance which produces forecasts that are too narrow in their distribution. That is, they tend to underestimate outcomes on both sides of the mean. See Barrero (2022).

There is more evidence suggesting a cautious approach towards forecasting financial performance. For instance, Stotz and Lu's (2015) study of equity analysts' earnings forecast accuracy in over 70 countries reveals that their 12-month earnings forecasts are rarely accurate. Covering a 12-year period, realized earnings per share have been, on average, just 80% of what was forecasted. These numbers highlight a large deviation between

[2] The expected value is calculated by multiplying the probability of each outcome by its corresponding value and summing these weighted values.

the base-case cash flows that firms tend to use when evaluating projects and what actually could be expected. In short, base-case scenarios tend to be too optimistic.

Benefits of Stress Tests

There is a strong correlation between financial markets and corporate cash flow generation. Hence, for many companies, an economic downturn is likely to result in decreased profitability and cash flows, as well as worsening financing options. One clear advantage of testing relevant stress variables is to gain better insight into their respective sensitivities to cash flows and funding requirements. After all, company management has an obligation to do what it can to prevent value-destroying events such as bankruptcy, issuing equity at distressed market prices, and cancelling or cutting dividends.

Capital Budgeting and Scenario Thinking

Many companies already use scenarios in their capital budgeting processes. Instead of employing different hurdle rates for various projects, they utilize the same cost of capital for all organic investments. However, they differentiate between the projects through in-depth scenario analysis. The objective of this process is not only to determine a probability-weighted Net Present Value (NPV) figure but also to establish a robust framework for a qualitative discussion regarding a potential investment. Cash flow modelling of scenarios, such as the base-case, best-case/worst-case scenarios, and various event cases, is incorporated into the discussion concerning strategic fit and risks. The latter part of the discussion typically centres on factors such as competitive position, geographical footprint, technological risks, cultural fit, and embedded real options.

Despite the significant role played by highly advanced scenario set-ups in the capital budgeting process for many companies, in our experience, this method has not yet become widely adopted as a practice for evaluating capital allocation and cash flow deployment options.

How to Think When Setting Up Scenarios

The most common set-up for companies is to construct three different scenarios as part of their planning process with the base case being complemented by a downside and an upside scenario. According to the Duke CFO survey (see Graham et al. 2013), companies often use downside scenarios for contingency planning where companies can prepare for potential cost reductions and other actions that mitigate the costs of distress. Upside scenarios are generally used as a tool for motivating employees.

When companies set up sensitivity scenarios, they typically focus on changes in variables like sales, gross margin, operating margin, working capital, investment costs, and currency.

For many companies, the historic data provides a good starting point when trying to get a feel for the sales and margin volatilities. But since every new economic crisis seems to be unique, some caution should be added to the use of historical data. The post pandemic inflation shock, for example, was not so much a stress on sales as it was on margins in general, and gross margins in particular. This time around, investors and market analysts became very focused on value drivers like pricing power, supply chain management, and "built-in" inflation hedges in customer contracts.

Having a profound understanding of the company's operational leverage and margin dynamics can help in scenario and stress tests by determining the extent to which costs can be adjusted in response to changes in revenue.

It is important to pay extra attention to the cash flow and working capital characteristics. During the global financial crisis, many companies experienced significant decreases in sales. However, the pressure on cash flow and liquidity was somewhat alleviated by the release of inventory and accounts receivables. For instance, the Swedish truck manufacturer Volvo released approximately SEK 20 billion in working capital during the period of 2008–2009, which was crucial for the company when it came to paying back maturing debt. Recently, we have seen an increasing number of companies using working capital as a source of funding for their operations. And for companies with negative working capital, the decline in free cash flow during a downturn will be exacerbated. The improvement they have made in their return on invested capital comes at a cost to liquidity. For these companies, it is especially important to stress-test cash flow and liquidity.

Another important test to make is to try to assess to what extent the company is "re-investible" during a downturn. If the return on invested capital stays at acceptable levels (close to or even above the cost of capital) even during cyclical lows, the likelihood is high that the company will return to a sound ROIC spread. And for those companies, the lenders and other stakeholders can be more certain about equity capital support from the owners, if need be.

The "reversed calculation" method is a powerful tool that can be used to address complex financial questions. It involves working backwards from a desired outcome to determine the input variables required to achieve that outcome. This approach is particularly useful when answering questions related to stress testing the business and its funding needs. For instance, consider the question of how severe a stress case the liquidity back-up facilities are covering for. Using the reversed calculation method, we can start by defining what constitutes a severe stress case, and then work backwards to determine the amount of liquidity that would be needed to cover this scenario. By conducting this exercise, managers can gain a better understanding of the company's liquidity needs and whether the current cash position and back-up facilities are a sufficient cover.

Similarly, the reversed calculation method can be used to determine how large a margin drop the company can withstand before getting downgraded to a non-investment grade rating. By working backwards from, for example, the desired rating level, managers can identify the margin levels that would trigger a downgrade, and then develop strategies to manage these risks.

Another example of the reversed calculation method in action is determining the maximum amount of debt that can be used to fund an acquisition or investment. By working backwards from, for instance, the desired debt to EBITDA level in a stress case, managers can identify the maximum amount of debt that can be used, while still maintaining a sustainable capital structure.

It is important to note that the process of stress testing and using the reversed calculation method is as much about the discussions and scenarios as it is about the numbers. By engaging in these exercises and discussions, managers can, for example, gain a deeper understanding of the relationship we reviewed in Chapter 9, namely that between business risk, capital structure, and funding.

Shareholder Activism

We end this chapter by briefly adopting a shareholder activism perspective in order to provide corporate decision-makers with some basic insights into how this group of investors thinks about value creation. The shareholder activist group is an especially interesting part of the investment community to study, as their engagement and willingness to challenge the status quo differentiate them from many other investors.

Shareholders may turn to activism if they believe it is an effective way to increase the value of a company. That might, for instance, include addressing corporate governance-related issues such as board and management composition, pay-out policies, or management remuneration. Other topics of interest for shareholder activism include corporate restructuring, the capital structure, and improving business operations. The ultimate goal of activism is to motivate management and boards to make changes in the way they run their companies.

According to Goldman Sachs (2023), US companies targeted by activist investors typically outperform their sectors initially, but the longer-term return patterns tend to be more ambiguous. However, an equal-weighted portfolio of all activist targets since 2006 has generated an average annual excess return relative to the Russell 3000 of 3 percentage points.

Thus, there are reasons why learning about shareholder activist strategies could be of interest for corporate management. Activists often scrutinize how companies allocate capital and advocate for efficient use of resources. Shareholder activists also tend to be very focused on actions that enhance shareholder value and reduce the principal-agency problem. So what are the main strategies deployed by activists when screening and approaching their targets?

In order to end up on an activist shortlist, companies most often *underperform* from a TSR perspective relative to their industry peers. *Large cash balances* and *recurring restructuring costs* add to the risk of getting on the list.

The Goldman Sachs report as well as an analysis conducted by Credit Suisse (2019) rank *conglomerates* as the top candidates for activist attention. According to Credit Suisse, if a company consists of five or more businesses, the risk of being approached by activists is four times as high compared to mono-line companies.

Other common focus areas among activist funds include *reviewing strategic alternatives*, blocking a proposed *merger or acquisition* or *becoming a target* of a potential acquisition.

It is hardly surprising to see which areas activist funds have been focusing on, given what we have learned so far in this book. In the Nordic space, we have witnessed several companies becoming targets for shareholder activists. For example, activist investor Cevian called for changes at the telecom company Ericsson in 2017. Cevian's campaign involved implementing cost-cutting measures and adopting a strategy focused more on core markets. Another instance was when the electrification and automation company ABB gave in to pressure from Cevian and sold its underperforming Power Grids unit to Hitachi in 2018. Lastly, it is worth mentioning Elliot Management's investment in Telecom Italia, which aimed to influence the company's corporate governance and advocate for better transparency. Elliot also pushed for cost reductions, network investments, and the divestment of non-core activities. (See the Elisa versus Telia case study.)

For management and boards that have the skill set, it could prove to be time well spent to proactively evaluate whether they may become an activist target. Hopefully, reading this book will, at least to some extent, facilitate such an evaluation. In Chapter 14, we will make a case study of the Swedish industrial company Sandvik, which can serve as inspiration as to how an activist-based evaluation, at least regarding the conglomerate aspect of shareholder activism, could look.

Conclusions

In this chapter, we have attempted to explore the benefits that an "Investor's mindset" could bring to an executive's capital allocation framework. We particularly highlight three areas where the investor community excels.

Firstly, any skilled investor needs to be aware and vigilant about behavioural shortcomings, such as loss aversion, overconfidence, and anchoring. These shortcomings could be mitigated by adopting a clear and rule-based approach to investing. For corporate managers, a **disciplined and rule-based approach** to capital allocation might involve asking questions about an investment's predefined stop-losses or fall-back plans. Other questions to consider could aim at mitigating negative effects stemming from overconfidence, such as competition neglect and a lack of the so-called outside view.

Secondly, we bring up the topic of **risk-reward trade-offs**, which is one of the most fundamental building blocks in investment theory. Risk is a relatively hard concept to understand and is further complicated by the uncertainty surrounding financial and economic distributions. One way to approach this challenge is by using expected value as a decision-making tool. It helps management in prioritizing and selecting investments or a portfolio of projects that offer the highest expected value, while considering the associated risks.

Thirdly, we review the benefits of using **scenario modelling**, which has been widely adopted among investors. Practicing contingency planning can help a company stay agile and be prepared for events coming its way. The most common set-up for companies is to construct three different scenarios as part of their planning process, with the base case complemented by a downside and an upside scenario. Another powerful technique that can be used in setting up scenarios is the "reversed calculation" method. This approach can be useful when trying to answer questions related to stress tests, such as the liquidity back-up needs, margin sensitivities to rating downgrades, or required ROIC levels for certain dividend pay-out levels.

Finally, we adopted a shareholder activist perspective on value creation and learned, among other things, the significance of addressing principal-agent costs for this group of investors. This could involve advocating for modifications to management's incentive programmes or questioning the corporate structure or strategy, such as the potential breakup of conglomerates.

References

Barrero JM (2022) The Micro and Macro of Managerial Beliefs. Journal of Financial Economics 143:640–667.

Credit Suisse (2019) Shareholder Activism: An Evolving Challenge. Published online. https://www.credit-suisse.com/us/en/investment-banking/ibcm/corporate-insights/shareholder-activism.html.

Goldman Sachs (2023) Do Activist Investors Boost Shareholder Returns? Published online. https://www.goldmansachs.com/intelligence/pages/do-activist-investors-boost-shareholder-returns.html.

Graham JR, Harvey CR, Puri M (2013) Managerial Attitudes and Corporate Actions. Journal of Financial Economics (109):103–121.
Kahneman D (2012) Thinking, Fast and Slow. Penguin Books Ltd.
Stotz A, Lu W (2015) Financial Analysts Were Only Wrong by 25%. Published online. https://papers.ssrn.com/sol3/papers.cfm?abstract_id=2695216.
Thorndike WN (2012) The Outsiders: Eight Unconventional CEOs and Their Radically Rational Blueprint for Success. Harvard Business School Publishing.

CHAPTER 12

Downturns Rearrange the Board

We now turn our attention to a subject closely related to stress scenarios and financial flexibility, namely that of recession management. It is well-known that downturns can represent a big threat to the financial health of a company. However, history has also shown that such periods can open up opportunities to leapfrog the competition. For the companies that manage to excel during a downturn, there is therefore much to win!

> *We plan for several scenarios in each of the divisions and at Group level. Even if the outlook of the general economic situation may appear bleak, we should also remember that every downturn also brings opportunities.*
> Cecilia Felton, CFO Sandvik (2022)

Sharp Divergence in Performance During the Downturn

A sign of an increased competitive volatility can be seen from the wide distribution in total shareholder return (TSR) during the Global Financial Crisis. While the majority of our sample of 160 Nordic companies delivered negative returns over the period 2006–2009, around a third managed to do the opposite.

T. Arenbo, *Capital Allocation and Value Creation*,
https://doi.org/10.1007/978-3-031-47048-6_12

Looking at the top quartile in our sample, the average annual TSR was above 4.8%. Although all companies in the top quartile did not return their cost of capital, they significantly outperformed the sample median (at −5.5% per year). The extraordinary wide spread in performance during the recession confirms findings from earlier studies on broader samples by, e.g. Bain & Company (2019) and McKinsey (2019).

Recession Winners Pulled Ahead and Excelled Also in the Post-recession Period

That companies are more or less cyclical is of course not news. This is, however, not the simple explanation to the pattern described above. First of all, a broad range of sectors are represented both among the recession winners and the losers. Moreover, there is no excess return pattern between the top quartile and the rest of the sample during the boom years leading up to the crisis.

When entering the downturn, however, the top quartile quickly pulled ahead and opened up a substantial performance gap. Interestingly enough, they also managed to extend the gap further during the post-recession period 2009–2012 (Fig. 12.1).[1]

Growth Was the Largest TSR Driver for Recession Winners

The big question is of course what the recession winners tend to do differently. While we will elaborate on conclusions from previous research in the next section, we can use a TSR decomposition on our Nordic sample for some initial guidance.

It shows that while margin improvement was an important factor for performance over the downturn, **by far the largest TSR driver for the top quartile was sales growth**. The recession winners managed to grow at a median annual rate of 9.6% versus 1.4% for the rest of the sample. When BCG (2019) did a similar analysis on companies that had managed to deliver an annual TSR of +10% during a downturn, the corresponding

[1] Around two-thirds of the top-quartile companies outperformed the sample median also in the post-recession period.

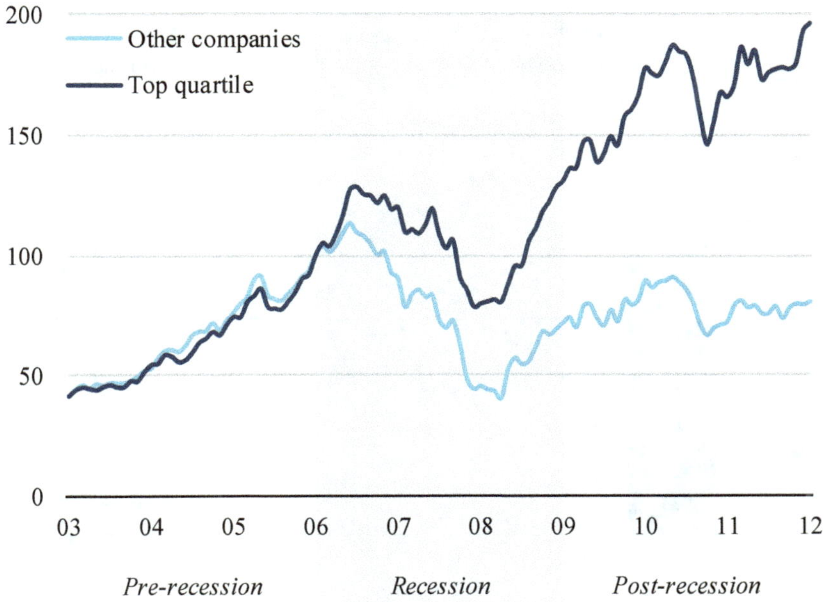

Fig. 12.1 Median TSR development (December 2003–December 2012)

numbers were 8.8% and 1.6%. In line with our findings, revenue growth had been the primary TSR driver for outperformers.

While all companies need to manage costs carefully during a downturn, it is thus evident that it is important to find a balance between such defensive moves and more offensive growth-supportive actions (Fig. 12.2).

Necessary to Move Past Survival Mode

Managing costs is a matter of self-preservation during a downturn. Focusing solely on cost-cutting has, however, historically shown to be a **losing strategy**. A study from Harvard Business Review (2010) found that the companies that followed such a defensive approach were least likely to outperform their rivals after a recession.

Part of the explanation to the underperformance is that arbitrary cost-cutting risks harming the company's future competitive power and

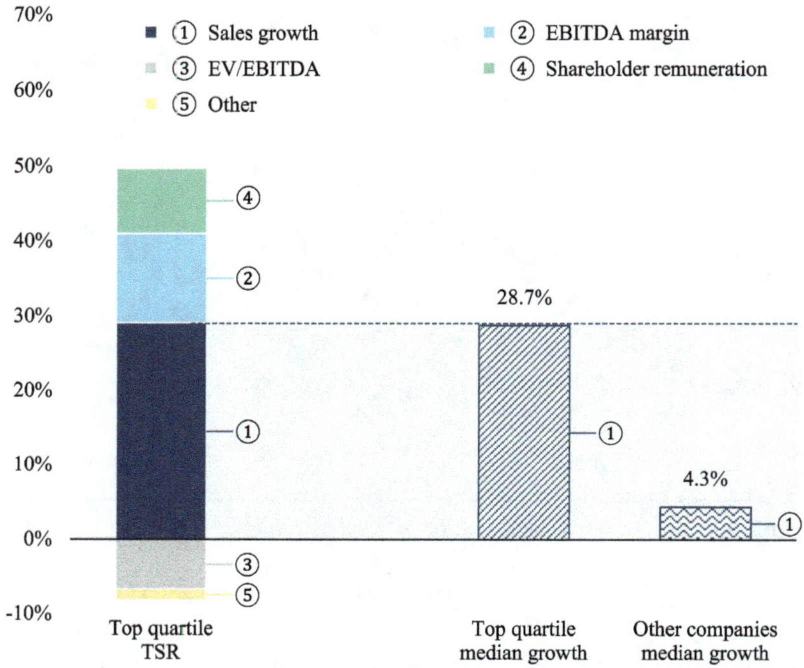

Fig. 12.2 TSR decomposition for our Nordic sample—yearly average (December 2006–December 2009)

long-term growth potential. For example, McKinsey (2007) has found that recession laggards tend to cut their R&D and advertising spending more, relative to their peers. Boston Consulting Group (2019) also shows that companies that favoured a short-term orientation during the global financial crisis underperformed on TSR.

Most studies find that **recession winners** instead tend to manage costs selectively taking into account their long-term impact. Rather than slashing across the board (incl. R&D, advertising spend, and/or headcount), outperformers tend to focus on costs that minimize the harm to future value creation. See for example Bain & Company (2019).

The timing of the savings programme also seems to be essential. BCG stresses that companies that end up cutting costs behind the curve are more likely to overcompensate. McKinsey finds that many successful companies proactively increased the flexibility of its cost base prior to the crisis.

During a Downturn, the Best Defence Can Be a Good Offensive

As mentioned, the opportunity to leapfrog the competition may be greater during downturns. While recession losers generally take a defensive stance, the winners do the opposite. Studies (including our own) show that the largest TSR driver for outperformers tends to be **top-line growth**.

One explanation is the tendency to act countercyclically when it comes to investments. For example, Bain and McKinsey (2002) find that while laggards scaled back on R&D and marketing during the recession, outperformers did not. As for capex, McKinsey concluded that the top quartile during the 2000 recession outspent the sample by 15%. These findings, as can be seen in Fig. 12.3, are confirmed by our Nordic sample as well.

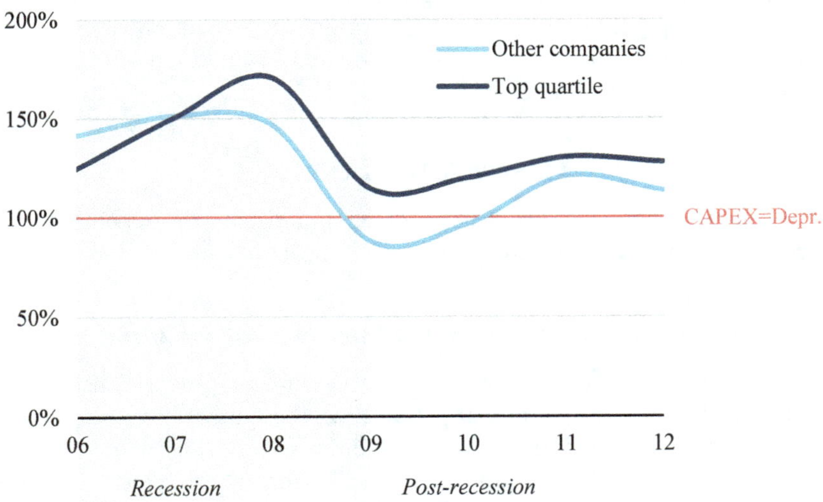

Fig. 12.3 Median CAPEX/depreciation ratio for our Nordic sample (2006–2012)

Many successful companies also used the downturn to initiate large-scale change. For some, this involved exiting non-core businesses. For others, it involved making strategic acquisitions at depressed valuations to grow the business. McKinsey found that while winners spent less on M&A during the pre-recession period (13% lower) they invested 7% more in M&A during the downturn.

A Solid Financial Footing

While an offensive capital allocation strategy is a common denominator among recession winners, preparation and financial discipline seem essential to be successful. Harvard Business Review concluded that relying purely on offensive actions (ignoring defensive ones) has usually not been a winning strategy.

But one of the most important takeaways from several of the research papers referred to in this chapter is the one about **financial flexibility**.

A company with a solid financial footing can more easily navigate through the fog of a crisis, where longer-term opportunity is both more abundant and obscured. This is highlighted in the graph, showing how our Nordic top-performing quartile had a debt-to-equity ratio of 0.15× coming into the global financial crisis compared to a median of 0.36× for the other three quartiles (Fig. 12.4).

Case Study: Lindab

The Lindab Group is a European producer and distributor of solutions in sheet metal and steel for construction and ventilation.

Equity Story and Business Case Leading Up to the Financial Crisis

The company has a history of high growth and margins and had been a very cash generating company up until the global financial crisis. The recession changed the market conditions, resulting in a substantial sales and EBITDA margin drop. The balance sheet rapidly became stretched following prior large cash outflows, contributing to a substantial underperformance compared to the peer group (Fig. 12.5).

As a result, Lindab initiated a number of cost reduction measures and became very focused on margin improvement, which most likely affected sales negatively. By decomposing the TSR during the years November

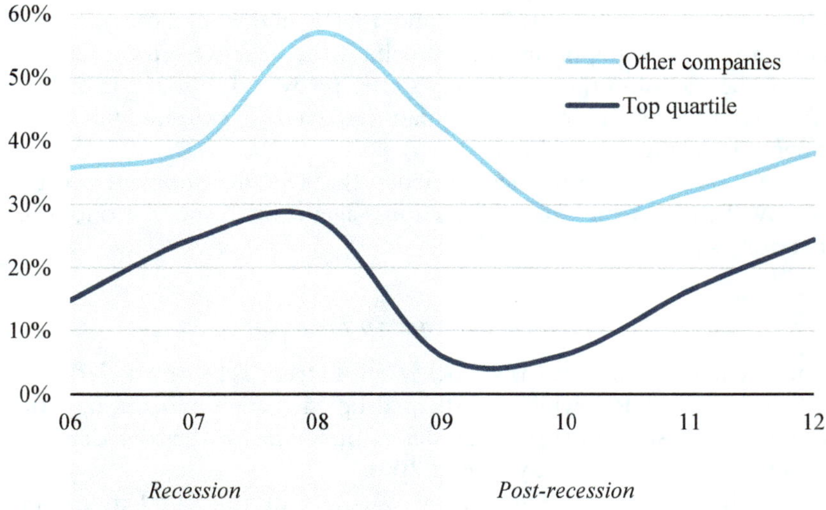

Fig. 12.4 Net debt/equity for our Nordic sample (2006–2012)

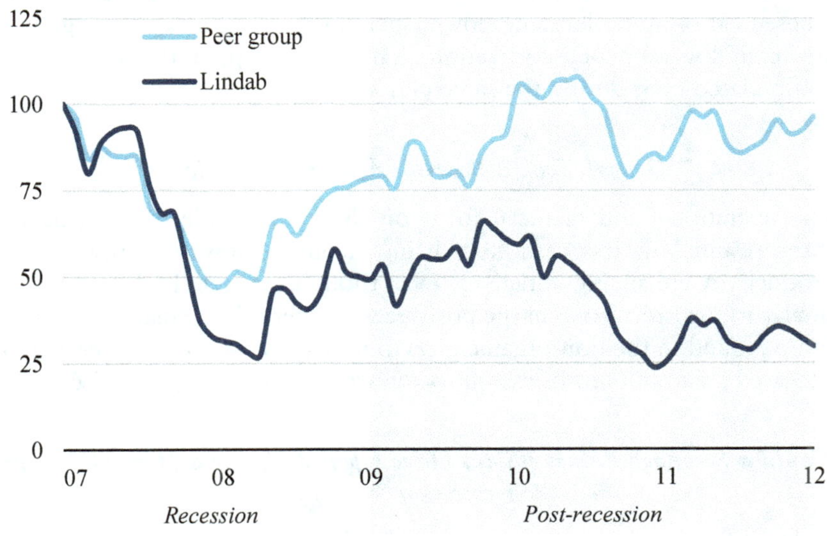

Fig. 12.5 TSR development for Lindab versus peers (November 2007–December 2012)

2007–2009 and 2009–2012, we find that a higher cyclicality in sales and margins were important factors behind the negative return. Coming out of the recession the peer group's sales recovered, but at the expense of lower margins. In contrast, Lindab defended its margins, but at the expense of losing sales volume.

The lack of growth further burdened the TSR development through the EV/EBITDA multiple contraction—again much more pronounced than for its peers.

Highest Leverage in the Sector

Lindab entered 2008 with a Net debt/EBITDA of 1.4× and a Net debt/EV of 15%. But following the sharp drop in market cap during 2008 together with substantial shareholder remunerations, the Net debt/EV ratio rose to above 40% at year-end 2008.

Lindab chose not to issue any new equity during 2009 in contrast to some of its peer companies with similar leverage. During the subsequent years, Lindab had the highest leverage among the peer companies, almost double the average in the group. And through 2009–2012, Lindab focused on bringing leverage down, spending around 50% of the generated cash flow on debt amortizations. The peer group, on the other hand, accumulated debt during the same period.

Growth Took a Beating After the Recession

The operational and financial focus on the liability side of the balance sheet resulted in less cash flow being deployed towards growth and productivity enhancing initiatives. Even though the scale-back in capex is similar to the peer group in the post-recession period, the main difference can be found in the non-organic growth initiatives, where the peer group allocated a fair amount of cash flow towards acquisitions (Fig. 12.6).

Could a Stronger Balance Sheet Have Opened Up for a More Offensive Post-recession Strategy?

Obviously, not all companies are hit in the same way by a downturn, but we believe Lindab was underinvested and too defensively focused during and after the global financial crisis. It is also plausible that the

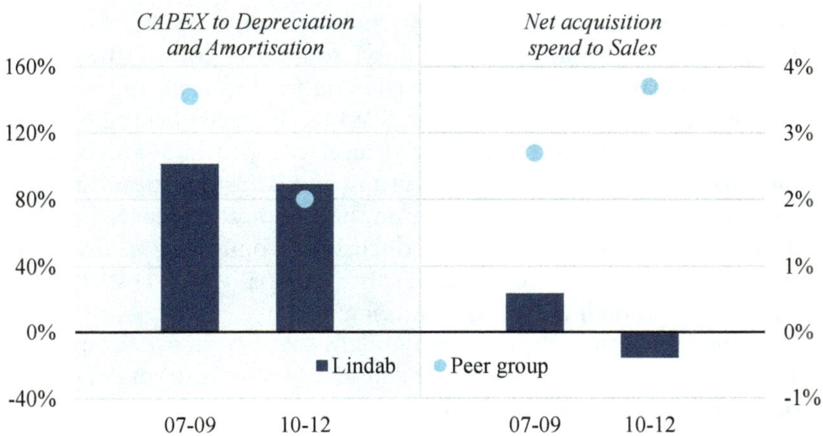

Fig. 12.6 CAPEX/depreciation and amortization and net acquisition spend to sales

cost-cutting focus had indirect negative spillover effects on soft factors like the corporate culture.

Once the balance sheet regained its strength, the CEO Ola Ringdahl, who took over in mid-2018, started to allocate more cash flow towards investments. In 2019, margins started to increase and in the following years, the stock strongly outperformed the peer group.

Conclusions

In this chapter, we have empirically tried to find clues as to how a company can come out of a recession as a winner. Our own study from the global financial crisis primarily highlights two differentiating factors between the winners and the rest of the group.

- The top quartile had a much stronger sales growth during, but also after, the downturn. It is worth noting that the difference did not exist before the crisis.
- The top quartile also had a much stronger balance sheet before and during the recession. On average the winners had a debt to equity of 0.15× compared to a median of 0.36× for the rest of the group.

Several international papers have been written on the subject of recession management showing very similar results. A lot of the factors explaining, at least part of the top quartiles outperformance, can be linked to the strategic flexibility of having a strong balance sheet. For many of the worst performers, the picture is reversed, with high indebtedness leading to too much focus on cost-cutting and debt reduction. Our case study of Lindab shed some extra light on the empirical evidence. The findings in this chapter complement the discussion around an optimal capital structure and add to arguments about the potentially high costs to value creation that too high a leverage can bring.

The findings in this chapter also highlight the importance for management to conduct scenario modelling and to have a long-term perspective in order to handle market and cash flow volatility.

References

Bain & Company (2019) Beyond the Downturn: Recession Strategies to Take the Lead. Published online. https://www.bain.com/insights/beyond-the-downturn-recession-strategies-to-take-the-lead/.

BCG (2019) Advantage in Adversity—Winning the Next Downturn. Published online. https://www.bcg.com/publications/2019/advantage-in-adversity-winning-next-downturn.

Harvard Business Review (2010) Roaring Out of Recession. Published online. https://hbr.org/2010/03/roaring-out-of-recession.

McKinsey on Finance (2007) Preparing for the Next Downturn. Published online. https://www.mckinsey.com/capabilities/strategy-and-corporate-finance/our-insights/preparing-for-the-next-downturn.

McKinsey Quarterly (2002) Learning to Love Recessions. Published online. https://www.inc.com/articles/2002/07/24348.html.

McKinsey Quarterly (2019) Bubbles Pop, Downturns Stop. Published online. https://www.mckinsey.com/capabilities/strategy-and-corporate-finance/our-insights/bubbles-pop-downturns-stop.

Sandvik (2022) Published online. https://www.home.sandvik/en/stories/articles/2022/11/resilience-through-agility/.

PART IV

Put It All Together

All three building blocks are now in place: the theoretical foundation, the cash flow deployment alternatives, and the investor toolbox. It is time to put our market based capital allocation framework together.

We start part 4 with a chapter discussing how important it is that a company's financial targets and key performance indicators are in line with the business strategy and the owners' risk preferences. After all, as an executive you manage assets on behalf of the owners, and hence your actions should align with the investors' objectives. Thus, a capital allocation framework should include financial targets and incentive programmes that improve the prospects of value creation as well as reduce the agency cost.

In the second chapter of this part, we conduct a case study where we aim to use the tools we have reviewed in order to extract information from the market. Thus we apply a practical, market-oriented approach in order to shed some light on the complex issues of capital deployment and the creation of shareholder value.

In the last chapter, we summarize the findings of the book in the form of a three-step capital allocation framework. The first step involves determining the relative importance of the three value drivers; ROIC, growth, and cost of capital. In the following step, decision-makers need to evaluate the available cash flow deployment alternatives with a risk and reward mind-set. The third and last step contains a practical guide to ways to think about capital allocation priorities and their attached financial targets.

CHAPTER 13

Financial Targets and Policies—Capital Allocation Priorities in Essence

As the CEO of a company, what message would you like to send to your organization and financial stakeholders, and why? The financial targets should align with the company's mission and strategy. Ideally, when determining the financial goals and their priorities, one should consider the key value drivers of the business.

However, in reality, the mission and strategy, as well as the attached financial goals, are sometimes not derived solely from a focus on value creation. One example that comes to mind is a CEO's excessive focus on growth. Another potential pitfall is the ambition to be everything for every investor when setting financial targets. It is important to ensure that the targets are coherent both internally and with the equity story. Incoherent targets, such as conflicting growth and dividend ambitions, can result in differing views among investors on how to allocate available capital between investments and dividends.

Another challenge in setting financial goals is adapting to changing economic and competitive environments. Financial priorities will change over time, and the financial targets must be adjusted accordingly. The Coloplast case study later in this chapter illustrates how this challenge can be addressed in practice.

T. Arenbo, *Capital Allocation and Value Creation*,
https://doi.org/10.1007/978-3-031-47048-6_13

Starting with Shareholder Feedback

Interaction with investors is a very direct way of understanding your stock valuation. A systematic approach to shareholder feedback can prove to be a valuable opportunity to improve equity market communication, as well as provide outside insight into the business strategy. In that sense, investor communication is as much about managers listening to the right kinds of investors, as it is about the company telling its story to investors.

But not all investors are equally important to listen to. Traders, retail investors, and index-tracking funds will probably not be able to provide you with the desired information and feedback. It will take a different, more informed kind of investor, the so-called intrinsic investor, typically found among pension funds and actively managed mutual funds. They are investors who are primarily focused on the long-term value and tend to be patient, buy-and-hold investors willing to weather short-term volatility to benefit from the long-term potential. Even though they lack experience in running a company, they likely have seen some CEOs fail at capital allocation and a few succeed. At the very least, they understand the financial markets, and their insights into value creation could provide valuable advice.[1]

In addition to intrinsic investors, management can benefit from a dialogue with sell-side analysts. However, sell-side analysts tend to follow the interests of the trading-generating investors, i.e. those with a shorter holding period focus. Even so, sell-side analysts are often very knowledgeable about the company and the sector in which it is active. They also benefit from speaking frequently with many of the most important investors in the company.

[1] Harford et al. (2018) study the effect of investor horizon and corporate decisions. They find that long-term investors strengthen governance and restrain managerial misbehaviours. Moreover, they discourage a range of investment and financing activities but encourage pay-outs and innovation. The authors claim that shareholders benefit through higher profitability as well as lower risk.

Financial Targets Should Express the Company's Ambition to Create Value

The strategy that management chooses to pursue, expressed in terms of value drivers, will likely be relatively stable over time and should, as such, show a high correlation with the historical performance drivers. The financial goals should, in turn, be coherent with the potential TSR drivers.

In theory, this might seem like a straightforward process. In practice, however, companies may lack sufficient knowledge about their true value drivers and how to prioritize between them. And as stated above, the CEOs' values and conviction, rather than the shareholders', might take the company in the wrong direction from a value creation perspective.

Case Study: A Telecom Company

A telecom company has long been focused on growth, supported by its financial targets and management incentive programme. For example, the company had a net sales growth target of 4–10% CAGR. Between 2012 and 2021, the company allocated capital to investments and acquisitions, spending over two-thirds of the generated cash flows from operations.

To achieve the growth initiatives, the company supplemented the growth target with a cash flow target (cash conversion >70%). However, rather than increasing profitability, the company achieved the target by releasing working capital. Over the 10-year period, the company reduced its working capital to sales ratio by almost 20%-points.

Surprisingly, the TSR analysis revealed that the sales growth did not contribute positively to shareholder value; in fact, its contribution was slightly negative. Despite this, the company pursued growth through multiple acquisitions and took on customer contracts with significantly higher margin risk. Consequently, the earnings quality suffered, leading to an increase in the cost of capital. Throughout much of the period, the company's ROIC did not reach the cost of capital, raising questions as to whether the company truly had a "license to grow".

The misaligned growth ambitions eventually resulted in the company having to make goodwill write-downs of over EUR 1.5 billion. The average yearly total shareholder return during the period was a meagre 2.2%, compared to a cost of capital of around 10%.

If the financial goals and incentive programme would have been coherent with the potential TSR drivers, the outcome would probably have looked quite different. Given the earnings volatility, and consequently very high cost of capital, it would probably have been more value creative for the company to focus on the core business. This, in turn, could actually have implied that shrinking, rather than growing sales would have been the way forward for the company. A model indicating how the company could link the value drivers to its financial targets is presented in Fig. 13.1.

The company changed, at least partially, its financial targets in 2017 when it introduced a margin target and downplayed the importance of growth. Since then, the company has managed to increase margins, and

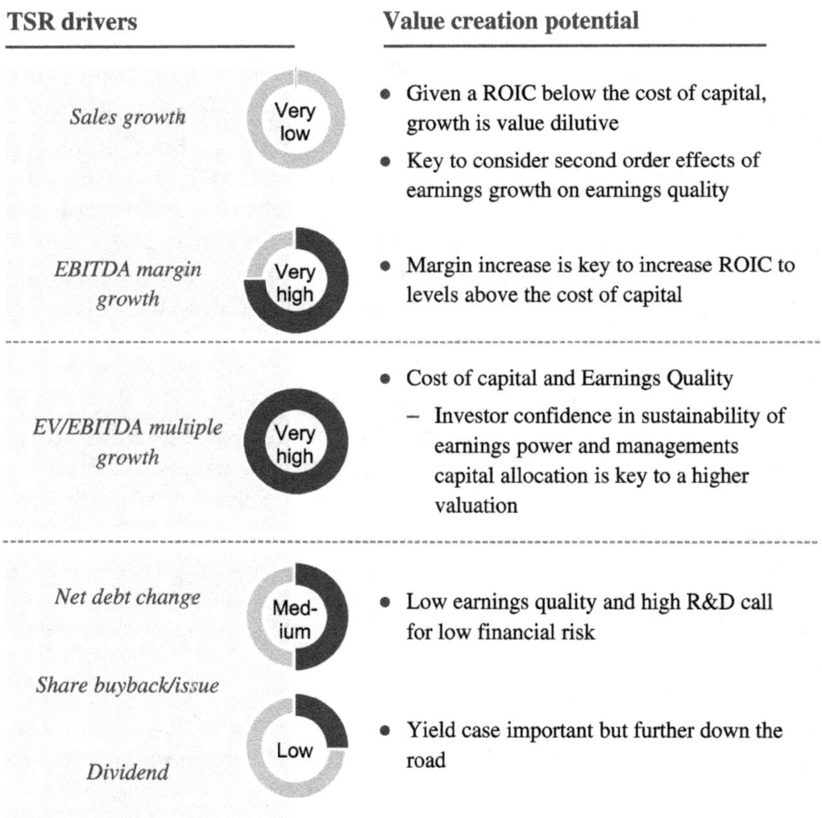

Fig. 13.1 Financial targets linked to value creation proposition

for the last couple of years, the ROIC has, with some margin, been above the cost of capital. During the period from 2017 and 2021, the company produced a strong annual average TSR of 15.2%.

Case Study: Church & Dwight

In this section, we draw inspiration from Church & Dwight, a consumer packaged goods company based in the United States that owns well-known brands such as Arm & Hammer and Trojan. The company has made a clear effort to link its TSR framework to its strategy and financial goals. They reached the conclusion that the gross margin was their main engine of cash flows and the most important value driver. Starting in 2005, the company's goal was to achieve high-quality growth, not just growth, through a transformation of its portfolio that targeted high-value brands and new product development. Acquisitions were also focused on growth that improved the gross margin and would maintain a strong multiple.

A special team addressed underperforming brands from a TSR perspective. The transformation resulted in fewer "Power Brands" with a more targeted marketing spend and a 5%-point increase in gross margins. Subsequently, a new financial policy increasing the focus on dividends was launched.

They tried to build a solid TSR framework where for example gross margins are not just the responsibility of operations, but everyone's responsibility. Additionally, the focus on operating income and Earnings Per Share (EPS) was replaced with a focus on value drivers, such as short and long-term trade-offs, the quality and volatility of revenue streams, the balance between margins and growth, and acquisitions evaluated using a discounted cash flow (DCF) model and a TSR framework, rather than just EPS accretion. A new incentive system was also put in place, linking operational improvements to the business unit's contribution to TSR.

The investor communication followed the TSR approach, explaining why one should invest in the company through a focus on gross margin, a selective M&A strategy, conversion of Free Cash Flow (FCF), and TSR-oriented management. The company has been true to its framework and in 2022 some of the key drivers of TSR mentioned were[2]:

[2] For the entire list of key TSR drivers see Company Annual Report 2022.

- **Focus on Power Brands**—while they sell over 80 brands, 14 of these brands generate over 85% of their revenues and profits
- **Focus on Gross Margin**—this fuels their organic growth and enables investments in marketing, research and development, and technology.
- **Superior Overhead Management**—adjusted SG&A is 13.6% of sales and 10.7% excluding amortization
- **Simple Incentive Compensation**—Bonuses are linked to four equally weighted drivers of TSR, including net sales growth, gross margin expansion, earnings growth, and operating cash flow.[3]

Despite operating in mature markets, the company managed to achieve a remarkable annual TSR of 17% between 2005 and 2022. The largest single driver of the TSR was the multiple expansion, which highlights the confidence the market has in the company's ability to uphold a high-earnings quality (Fig. 13.2).

Capital Allocation Priorities

In contrast to many US corporations, it is less common in Europe to see clearly defined financial target priorities. However, having clear priorities is crucial in the process of allocating capital, as it helps to avoid potential misallocations when conflicting goals are present.

As could be seen in the case study of **Carlsberg**, in Chapter 3, the company operates primarily in stable and mature markets. After several years of mediocre performance, the company launched a new strategy in 2016 with clearly stated goals and key performance indicators. The targets were structured with a priority for capital allocation, starting with organic profitable growth. The second priority was to maintain a NIBD/EBITDA ratio of less than 2.0× and the third priority was to allocate capital to shareholders through a dividend pay-out ratio of 50%. Any remaining excess cash was to be redistributed through buybacks or extraordinary dividends.

Electrolux a leading global appliance company has developed a goal set-up where they focus on the prerequisites for investing in growth. They

[3] In 2023, the company will add a fifth component, "Strategic Initiatives" that entails of: Digital Acceleration, International Expansion, Sustainability, Diversity & Inclusion, and Acquisition Integration.

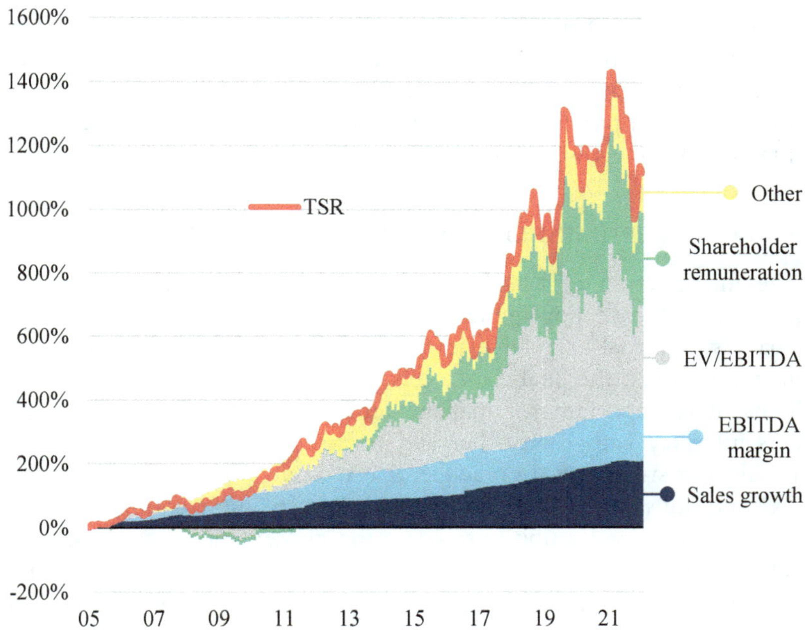

Fig. 13.2 TSR decomposition (Dec 2005–Dec 2022)

strive to achieve a return on net assets of >20% by delivering an operating margin of >6% and a capital turnover of >4×. The growth target is set to 4% with a solid capital structure target (net debt/EBITDA < 2×) and a dividend pay-out target of 50%.

However, Electrolux recognizes that growth must be profitable. To achieve this, they have implemented a three-step model. Firstly, they ensure that the business operates with a clear focus on stability and predictability. Secondly, the business model must be resilient to external factors and possess a clear competitive advantage to ensure long-term profitability. Finally, growth can be accelerated in a targeted way by leveraging its strength through selective investments. Thus, Electrolux has clearly identified the importance of both profitability and earnings quality as the most important value drivers and a prerequisite for growth.

Pandora, a successful Danish jewellery company, has a cash usage priority that starts with maintaining a solid balance sheet. Second priority is to invest in profitable organic growth. Next comes dividends, followed by share buybacks. Notably, inorganic growth is not included in their list of priorities. This decision is driven by the fact that the company's organic growth relative to the market is already substantial, and pursuing acquisitions could potentially divert management's focus from the highly profitable organic growth strategy.

The "Self-Sustaining" Model

In the introduction of this book, we briefly describe the "corporate eco-system" of cash flow generation and cash flow deployment. In a company's "internal" capital market, the inflows and outflows must be balanced—as must the financial targets.

Thus, it is important for management to understand how different targets interplay with each other and to assess whether the targets are financially self-sustaining. In practice, that typically boils down to whether ROIC and subsequent cash flow generation are high enough to fund growth and dividend ambitions, given the chosen capital structure. An imbalanced set of targets may indicate a reliance on funding from the capital markets, which may not be ideal for long-term stability. Based on our experience, most managers prefer to minimize their dependence on the sometimes unpredictable capital markets.

There is a rather straightforward way of testing whether the financial goals are in balance from a funding perspective. Building on the relation between ROIC and growth we can get the required reinvestment rate given no dividends or debt funding. In order to add the latter two factors we use a formula[4] originally developed by Donaldson (1985), which includes in total five variables: ROIC, growth rate, leverage, interest rate, and dividend pay-out ratio.

Typically, shareholders receive what remains after meeting growth aspirations and capital structure requirements. Hence, we want to know the self-sustaining pay-out ratio given a target growth rate of 5%, a debt-to-equity leverage of 25%, and a 3% interest rate environment. The line in Fig. 13.3 represents a balanced pay-out ratio for various ROIC levels.

There are more rigorous ways of testing whether the financial targets are coherent and financially self-sustaining, but this will provide an easy way to think about it. It also becomes very visible that a financial target

[4] Earnings-retention rate = Growth target / (ROIC + Leverage * (ROIC-interest rate)).

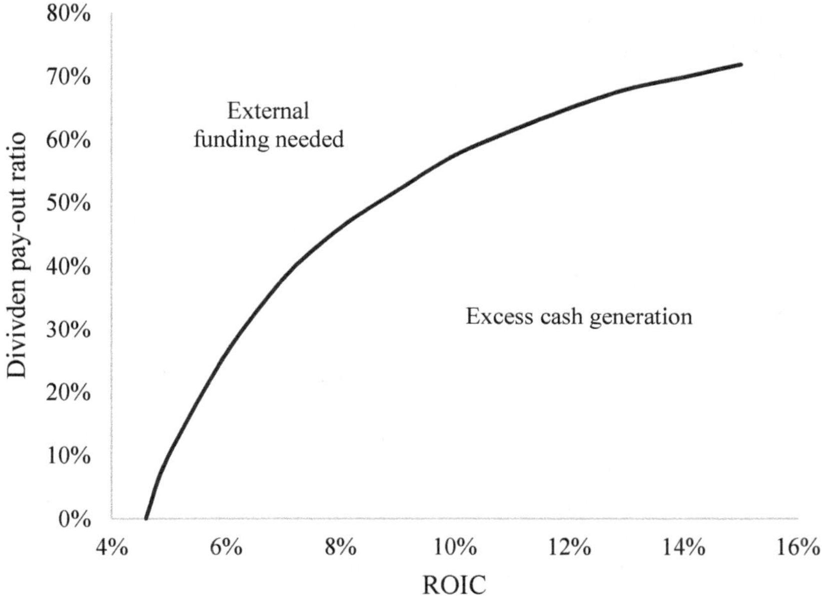

Fig. 13.3 Balanced pay-out ratio given a growth target of 5%

cannot be changed without taking into consideration how it will impact other goals and their funding.

Pros and Cons with Different Targets

Once a company has decided upon a strategy and which areas to prioritize, specific targets must be chosen. There are a few things that can be helpful to keep in mind when considering the different targets. For example, when it comes to **growth targets**, be aware of the risk of trading higher growth for lower earnings quality (as was the case in the telecom sector example). Another similar pitfall with growth targets is if they come at too high a price, which typically can take place if the growth ambitions are linked to an acquisition strategy. Furthermore, an unbalanced growth focus might hinder value-creating activities, such as divesting underperforming assets or spinning off parts of the operations.

And maybe most importantly, growth should only be made a priority if the firm's profitability allows it.

What should we look out for when it comes to the **EBIT-margin target?** One risk is that the capital need is ignored and projects with below target margins are put aside despite positive economic value added. Furthermore, one might miss the aspect of earnings quality—a lower and stable margin can be more valuable than a higher and more volatile margin.

Return on invested capital targets gives a clear focus on value adding investments/acquisitions. However, an asset base perspective must be added to the pure percentage-based ROIC-level target. Thus a "dollar" focus must be attached to a "margin" focus, i.e. what is the absolute amount of value created?

Over-allocation and migration towards riskier projects can pose a risk in connection to pure ROIC targets. To mitigate this risk, firms should not focus on ROIC as a stand-alone metric, but rather on ROIC in excess of the project's risk-adjusted cost of capital.

The flip slide to this risk is under-allocation, which can take place if the historic ROIC hurdle is too high. Again, decision-makers should focus on returns relative to risk, rather than the average ROIC, to create value for shareholders.

Return on Equity (RoE) targets also come with some challenges. For example, one risk is that positive economic value added projects may be rejected due to a lower RoE than the current level of the group. RoE does not take into account the capital structure or earnings quality, leading to a potential overemphasis on earnings per share (EPS) and potential debt-funded acquisitions. Debt-funded acquisitions at low interest rates that increase EPS may still be a very poor indicator of true value creation. Another challenge with an RoE target is the risk for management to be too short-term focused, which may result in underinvestment in areas such as sales, marketing, and research and development.

What **leverage target** should be selected? Balance sheet based targets like debt to equity or equity to assets might, as we pointed out in the capital structure chapter, be poor indicators of true balance sheet risk. Some companies choose to express their leverage target by linking it to a public rating. A goal that states a company's ambition, for example, to obtain a solid investment grade rating is obviously sending a strong signal to the market. However, by relying on an external part for your leverage target, you are putting some of the decisions beyond your own control.

For most sectors, we prefer to use cash flow based goals like net debt/EBITDA or operating free cash flow to net debt.

Cash flow targets are not commonly found among explicitly stated financial goals, with the exception of various cash conversion targets such as free cash flow to net profits. However, these cash conversion targets can be difficult to interpret, as they are heavily impacted by the current cash flow costs of growth, such as capital expenditures and changes in working capital, in comparison to historical depreciation costs. As a consequence, there are some risks attached to purely defined cash flow goals. One of these risks was previously mentioned, where a company in the telecom sector used financial engineering to release large amounts of tied-up working capital, making their balance sheet more vulnerable. Another potentially more significant risk is related to insufficient investment in both tangible and intangible asset in part stemming from an exaggerated short-term focus. Usually, the cash flows will follow the ROIC level and, given a sufficiently high ROIC, the cash flow will in most cases resolve itself over time.

Shareholder remuneration targets often come last in the cash flow prioritization order, but a majority of the listed companies state a dividend target expressed as share of net profit. The dividend target is sometimes complemented by a share buyback ambition, often more flexible in nature. A share buyback programme increases RoE but is sensitive to timing and is often done when times are good and share price is high. In practice that implies a risk of benefitting the sellers but hurting the remaining shareholders.

Earnings Quality—The Missing Piece of the Target Puzzle

In this book, we have emphasized on several occasions the crucial role that earnings quality plays in valuation. However, it appears to be a missing element of the financial targets puzzle. No financial target seems to align with earnings quality in the same way as the other two value drivers, growth and profitability do. The only targets we have seen used in this context are a margin interval target, where the companies state both a minimum and maximum margin target, and, on one occasion, also a margin volatility target (Fig. 13.4).

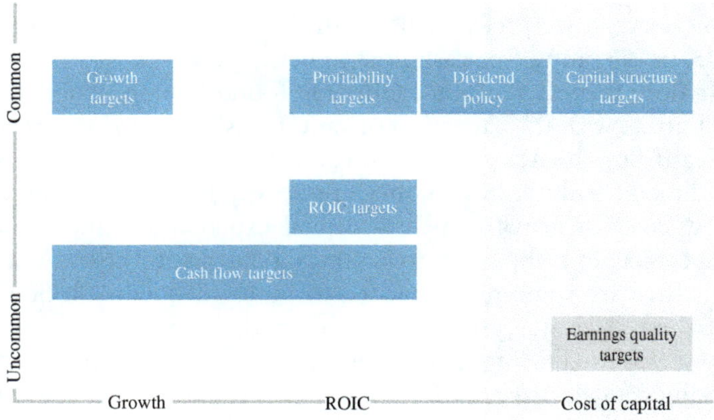

Fig. 13.4 Financial targets overview linked to the three value drivers

Difficulties with Earnings Quality Targets

Measuring earnings quality is complex, which makes it challenging for companies to establish clear and meaningful targets. For example, there is a lack of a clear definition, as well as the necessary data required to measure earnings quality. Moreover, since no clear standard has been established for measuring earnings quality, the lack of comparability between companies may make it more difficult for investors to interpret such a target.

Furthermore, improving earnings quality is a long-term process that requires a commitment to making changes spanning over many years. There may be a lack of incentives for companies to set outright targets for earnings quality specifically, as this type of target can only be tied to financial performance in the long term.

These are some of the reasons why targets linked to earnings quality are rare. However, as the volatile inflation environment makes investors increasingly interested in the quality of a company's earnings, it is possible that more companies will start to explore the possibility of setting targets in this area as well.

Risk with Unbalanced Targets

While growth and margin targets are important components of shareholder value creation, they should not be pursued without taking the aspect of earnings quality into the equation. What may the risks be of having incentives and financial targets linked to margin and sales goals but not to earnings quality?

- Earnings quality is only measurable in the long run, and a lack of awareness and appreciation of this value driver can lead to a short-term focus.
- Companies may prioritize achieving margin and growth targets at the expense of typical earnings quality factors, such as margin resilience and sales predictability.
- A less pronounced risk, nevertheless occasionally seen, is that companies may engage in aggressive accounting practices to inflate margins in the short term, for instance, through aggressive capitalization of R&D expenses.

Earnings Quality in a KPI and Incentives Setting

Although it can be difficult to link earnings quality to a specific financial target, there are other ways to incorporate and emphasize the concept of risk into a company's overall governance and incentive system. In contrast to a financial target, an incentive programme can be based on a more complex set of non-financial performance targets that are aligned with the company's strategic objectives.

Typically, the performance-based incentive programme is linked to employees' KPIs, which in turn are aligned with the company's strategic objectives. These KPIs may include proxy markers for earnings quality, such as a focus on gross margins, customer satisfaction scores, product quality measures, innovation targets, and brand recognition. As KPIs primarily have an internal focus and, as such, are not aimed towards external stakeholders, they are typically not disclosed as clearly as the financial targets are. However, below we give a few examples of some non-financial KPIs that companies mention in connection with incentive programmes.

For example, Atlas Copco's non-financial targets for sustainable growth include five priorities: ethical behaviour, health and safety, competent teams, resource efficiency, and innovation. See Atlas Copco (2016).

Novo Nordisk (2022) has several non-financial KPIs aligned with its purpose of driving change to defeat diabetes and other serious chronic diseases such as obesity, haemophilia, and growth hormone deficiencies. These KPIs include, among others, the number of patients reached, and the number of new products and services developed to address unmet medical needs.

And finally, the renewable materials company Stora Enso (2022) measures non-financial metrics through a balanced scorecard and includes targets for strategic areas such as innovation, customer insight, and motivated employees.

TSR Rooted Targets That Changed Over Time—Coloplast Case Study

We will now examine a case study of the Danish med-tech company Coloplast. The management and board of the company have effectively aligned its financial goals with the shareholder value drivers and have been able to adjust these targets in response to changing circumstances on the route towards superior value creation.

Stage 1-Growth at Any Price

After a prolonged period of innovation and growth, Coloplast encountered slowing organic growth (although from high levels) and declining profitability in the mid-2000s. The business model was impacted by various external factors such as healthcare reforms in the EU and increased competition, as well as **weak internal focus** such as:

- An unbalanced focus on revenue growth and an acceptance of underperformance within business areas and regions
- A weak link between strategy and execution
- Unsatisfactory cost levels and a lack of efficient "go to market" structure
- The DKK 15bn organic growth target (CAGR of around 10–11%) set out in 2005/2006 represented a growth pace of around

1.5–2.5× the underlying market growth thus requiring substantial market share gains over the period

Stage 2-Balanced Profitable Growth Strategy

As a result of the unbalanced growth strategy, the profitability took a hit and in 2006 the ROIC had dipped below the cost of capital. TSR for the period struggled to reach positive numbers.

As a result of the poor performance, a new strategy was developed in 2007/2008 and the equity story was updated highlighting **profit as a prerequisite for growth.** The turnaround resulted in an astonishing 32%-point ROIC increase over a five-year period mainly stemming from an EBIT-margin expansion. Important restructuring measures to raise the margin included (in addition to an overall simplification of the business):

- New financial targets included a **raised margin target** combined with a **less rigid growth target** and a lower Net debt/EBITDA target range
- Transfer of production to low-cost countries combined with an FTE reduction (gross margin expanded from below 60% to 67%)
- Further optimization of the cost structure through, for example, improved efficiency in back-office, the establishment of a shared service centre in Poland, and a simplified sales subsidiaries organization (the administration cost to sales ratio was cut into half going from 12% to around 6%)
- At the same time, Coloplast remained a top quartile spender within the healthcare sector when it came to sales and marketing activities, laying a strong foundation for continued profitable growth.

During the first period of the Coloplast "turn-around" journey, the TSR was mainly driven by margin expansion, which accounted for almost two-thirds of share performance. Despite the increased focus on profitability, the annual sales growth reached an impressive 6.5%. However, it is worth noting that it often takes time to build market confidence, which is demonstrated in Fig. 13.5 by the lack of valuation multiple expansion.

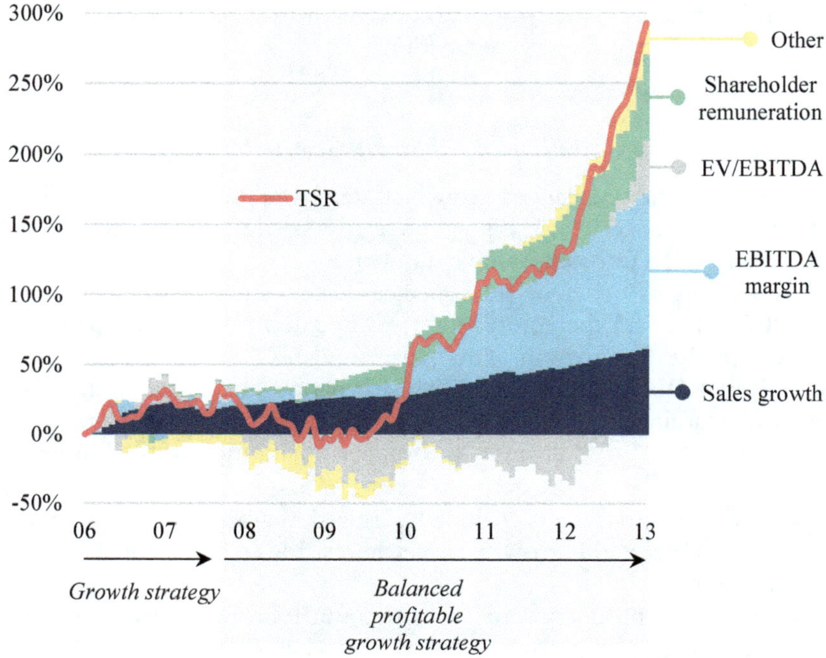

Fig. 13.5 Coloplast TSR decomposition (Dec 2006–Dec 2012)

Stage 3-Back to a More Rigid Growth Target

After successfully completing the turnaround in 2011/2012, Coloplast implemented a new global strategy and revised its equity story by prioritizing investments in growth and maintaining cost discipline. Over time, Coloplast became more stringent in its pursuit of growth, setting an annual organic growth target of 7–10% in 2013/2014. During this period, Coloplast also shifted its focus from expanding margins to maintaining a minimum level of margins, allowing for growth that may dilute margins but still create value.

The high ROIC has also facilitated an **increased pay-out ratio** over time. The initial 30% pay-out target, combined with a net cash position, may appear to be fairly conservative in hindsight. Communication indicated a desire to maintain flexibility for inorganic growth opportunities. However, since no significant merger and acquisition activities took place, the pay-out policy was adjusted so that all free cash flow became eligible for distribution to shareholders. This was manifested in the implementation of a pay-out target range of 80–100% in 2015/2016 (Fig. 13.6).

Notable for the second period is the significant multiple expansion resulting from a high and stable ROIC and a high confidence in the managements capital allocation priorities. Over the entire period, we estimate that the cost of capital decreased from 9% to approximately 6%, which played a significant role in the appreciation of the share price.

The Coloplast case study demonstrates how a TSR driven goal framework can be effectively implemented and achieved. The company not only found the ideal balance between growth and profitability, but it also managed to align its operations and financial goals. The result was a remarkable annual TSR of 16.2% between 2007 and 2022.

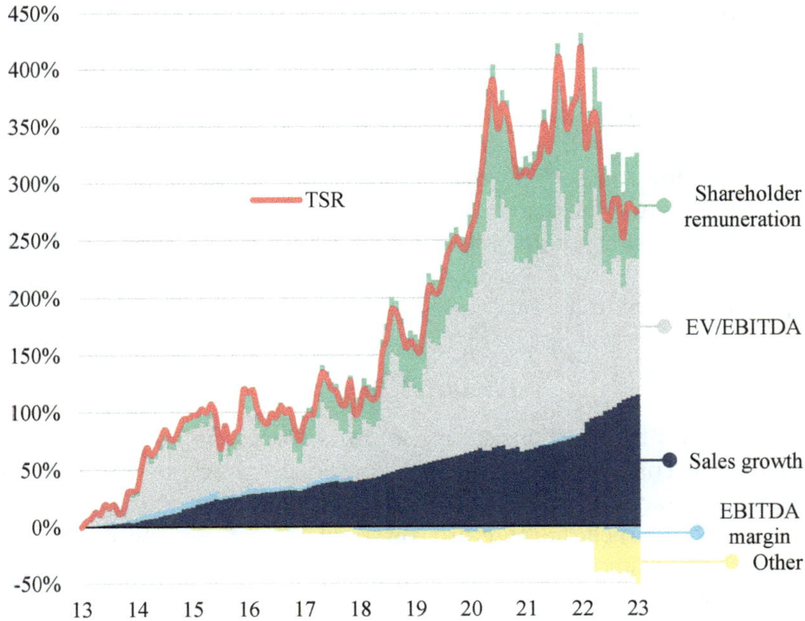

Fig. 13.6 Coloplast TSR decomposition (Dec 2012–Dec 2022)

Business Strategy and Financial Targets—Atlas Copco Case Study

In this section, we will briefly introduce how the business strategy and earnings quality can be linked to a TSR framework. We do it in the form of a case study of the Swedish industrial company Atlas Copco. Atlas Copco is a multinational industrial company that operates in various markets, including compressed air and gas equipment, as well as vacuum solutions. Atlas Copco is renowned for its strong focus on creating shareholder value and has achieved an impressive annual TSR of almost 20% in the 10-year period ending in 2022.

Business Strategy

We have chosen to categorize business strategy similarly to how we did in Chapter 4 about earnings quality. For a more complete review, please refer to the appendix. However, to summarize, the strategies we include are cost leadership, differentiation, market niche, diversification, and blue ocean.

A cost leadership strategy aims to become the low-cost producer in its industry, while a differentiation strategy aims to create unique and superior products or services that command a premium price. A market niche strategy involves targeting a specific segment of the market, while a diversification strategy involves expanding into new markets, products, or services. Lastly, a blue ocean strategy involves creating a new market space that is uncontested by existing competitors.

Financial Targets

When it comes to the financial targets, Atlas Copco has clearly communicated goals concerning its growth ambition (8% yearly over a business cycle) and dividend policy (50% of net profit). In addition, the company aims at a "sustained high return on capital" without specifying any numbers. There are no publicly communicated targets concerning the capital structure, nor is there any clearly stated priority between the capital allocation alternatives.

Mapping the TSR to the Group-Wide Components of the Business Strategy

We will now attempt to evaluate the extent to which Atlas Copco's business strategy aligns with its financial targets and historical drivers of shareholder value (Fig. 13.7).

Growth has been the single most contributing factor to Atlas Copco's total shareholder return since 2013. Several crucial components of the business strategy can be directly linked to this important value driver.

Atlas Copco operates in a *decentralized organization* where flexibility and best practices are prioritized over synergies and scale advantages. This flexible and diversified structure supports an entrepreneurial and growth-oriented business culture.

The company utilizes a *differentiation strategy* to target and expand its existing products and services into adjacent markets. This strategy is

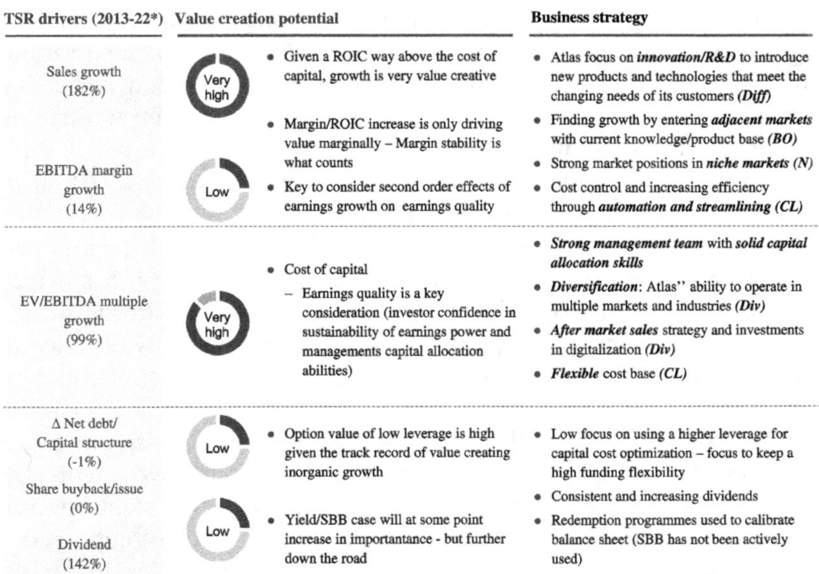

Fig. 13.7 Atlas Copco's TSR drivers in a value creation and business strategy context (*Note*: CL = Cost Leadership, Diff = Diffrentiation, Div = Diversification, N = Niche, BO = Blue Ocean (*) Including the spin-off of Epiroc)

facilitated by a strong focus on innovation. Atlas Copco invests heavily in research and development to introduce new products and technologies that meet the evolving needs of its customers.

The second most significant factor is the increase in **valuation multiple**, which to a large extent can be attributed to the cost of capital and ultimately the earnings quality of the company. Atlas Copco recognizes the importance of this value driver and has implemented an explicit strategy to maintain strong market positions in *niche segments*. This strategy enables the company to have a high pricing power which, in turn, improves margin stability and earnings quality.

A high share of *aftermarket sales* is another vital component in the strategy for Atlas Copco that underpins sales as well as margin stability. The service operations account for some 35% of total revenue and allow the company not only to bring down the volatility in an inherently cyclical sector, but also to stay in a close and ongoing dialogue with the customer.

Another significant factor, contributing to shareholder value and reflecting earnings quality, is the company's strong emphasis on *controlling costs and enhancing efficiency*. Atlas Copco has implemented various cost-saving measures such as streamlining its operations and decreasing overhead costs. Additionally, the company has invested in automation and digitalization to enhance efficiency and reduce costs. To better withstand cyclical end markets, the company aims to have around 10% of its workforce employed on flexible terms.

Furthermore, Atlas Copco has a *diversified* business model, with operations in multiple markets and industries. This diversification has helped the company to mitigate the impact of economic downturns in any one specific product or geographical market. However, as we learned in Chapter 6, diversification can be a double-edged sword when it comes to value creation and earnings multiples. In order to avoid a conglomerate discount, an effective capital allocation must be pursued. Atlas Copco has a disciplined approach to capital allocation and prioritizes investments that are aligned with the company's strategic objectives. A consistent business strategy across the entire organization mitigates the risk of a conglomerate discount and helps management to keep focus on the most important value drivers.

Atlas Copco has a strong track record of **returning capital to shareholders** through primarily dividend payments. However, historically the ROIC level has not only produced enough cash flow for the average annual 9% growth rate and 50% dividend pay-out ratio, but has been high enough in order to allow for three larger share redemption programmes between 2012 and 2022.

Finally, and with the least priority among value drivers, we find the capital structure—and rightfully so. There may come a time when leverage, in combination with dividends and share buybacks, will play a more important role in the value creation process. However, for that to happen, Atlas Copco must first run out of profitable growth options.

Case Study Summary

Given the high level of confidence in Atlas Copco's management in the market, they can afford to set relatively relaxed financial targets, except for growth. The strong organic growth and high-earnings quality have been the major drivers of the shareholder return where a clear link to the business strategy can be seen. Growth is underpinned by Atlas Copco's outspoken niche and differentiation strategy with a high focus on innovation. Additionally, sales are strengthened by its decentralized organization and entrepreneurial culture. Earnings quality benefits from a high share of aftermarket sales as well as a high pricing power, partly emanating from market-leading positions in niche markets. Moreover, the company has managed to reduce earnings volatility thanks to a successfully deployed diversification strategy. One reason Atlas Copco has been successful in running a conglomerate is the consistency in business strategy and value drivers across the four business units and 21 divisions.

Conclusions

Properly chosen financial goals should be based on a company's prospect to generate value. To evaluate the strategy, the historical TSR decomposition can be a valuable tool and a good starting point for increasing self-awareness regarding the company's value drivers.

Different industries have varying appropriate targets and ways of prioritizing them. Due to the trade-off between the three value drivers, the optimal financial goals of two companies in the same industry can also differ. For instance, if the ROIC is close to the cost of capital, the added benefit of increasing margins will be greater than the benefit of increased growth. However, if the ROIC spread is large, the relative benefit of growth will be much higher. This difference should be reflected in the chosen financial targets and their prioritization.

It is common to see companies setting "profitable growth" as its top priority target. Unfortunately, all too often it turns out to be empty words where profitable seems to be put second in priority to growth. For many companies, it would likely be much better if the words were separated and profitable came as a stand-alone first priority, with the growth target being contingent on the profitability target being accomplished. And, as we saw in the examples of Electrolux and Church & Dwight, they took it one step further and required growth not just to be profitable, but to be of "high quality" as well. Setting a growth target at low single digits does not have to translate into a low TSR, on the contrary.[5]

When it comes to the priority of financial targets and cash flow deployment, many companies fall short. However, to set a clear priority for the financial targets and the subsequent capital allocation is important for several reasons. For instance, setting clear priorities can give management a framework for evaluating investment opportunities and help in focusing its resources on the most critical initiatives. Moreover, clear priorities also improve communication within the company as well as with external stakeholders and help to ensure that everyone understands the company's strategic direction.

Another point about targets that is important to stress is that they are coherent and self-sustaining. In most cases, this is not a big problem, but if growth ambitions are high and external funding is required, this can lead to conflicts. For example, a growth target of 8% may not be commensurate with an investment grade rating and a dividend pay-out ratio of 50%.

The most commonly used targets include having a margin target and a growth target, followed by goals directed towards the pay-out ratio and capital structure. However, targets aimed at earnings quality are seen only on rare occasions. While growth and margin targets are important components of shareholder value creation, focusing too heavily on these targets at the expense of earnings quality can be very costly in terms of value creation in the long run. One way to overcome the lack of targets for

[5] Two American food companies, Flower foods and General Mills, can serve as inspiration and good examples of companies with low-growth targets and excellent long-term shareholder returns. Flower Foods has a sales growth target of 1–2% and achieved a growth CAGR of 4% and an annual TSR of 10% between 2013 and 2022. The corresponding numbers for General Mills were 2–3%, 1%, and 11.2%.

earnings quality is to explicitly link the value driver to a company's business strategies, as was highlighted in the Atlas Copco case study. "Best practice" is probably to have an "organizational culture of understanding" around the business strategy and the implicit and explicit links to the drivers of value—including that of earnings risk.

References

Atlas Copco (2016) https://www.atlascopcogroup.com/en/media/corporate-press-releases/2016/20161115-kpis.

Donaldson G (1985) Financial Goals and Strategic Consequences. Harvard Business Review.

Harford J, Kecskés A, and Mansi S (2018) Do Long-Term Investors Improve Corporate Decision Making?. Journal of Corporate Finance 50: 424–452.

Novo Nordisk (2022) https://www.novonordisk.com/content/dam/nncorp/global/en/investors/irmaterial/annual_report/2023/novo-nordisk-remuneration-report-2022.pdf.

Stora Enso (2022) https://www.storaenso.com/-/media/documents/download-center/documents/annual-reports/2022/storaenso_annual_report_2022.pdf#page=116.

CHAPTER 14

An Investor-Based Evaluation Process

We began this book by stating that, in order to effectively run a company, being a competent businessperson alone is not enough. It is also necessary to possess the skills of a knowledgeable investor, including the ability to read the market. In this chapter, we apply a practical, market-oriented approach to shed some light on the complex issues of capital deployment and the creation of shareholder value.

More specifically, our market-based evaluation process involves answering the following questions:

- What are the main drivers of Total Shareholder Return?
- What do the capital allocation priorities and historical cash flow deployment look like?
- What are the current market expectations embedded in the valuation multiple?
- What does an "optimal" capital structure look like, given the capital allocation priorities?
- How can the capital allocation and financial targets be communicated to the market?

T. Arenbo, *Capital Allocation and Value Creation*,
https://doi.org/10.1007/978-3-031-47048-6_14

We will highlight how a market and investor-based evaluation process can be conducted by using a case study of the large Swedish industrial company Sandvik. The company has a global reach with sales of more than EUR 10 billion. Sandvik has recently spun off one of its business units and is now organized into three remaining divisions.

What are the Main Drivers of Total Shareholder Return?

We begin by asking what the historical drivers of shareholder value have been and whether actual value creation aligns with the company's strategy. First, we want to determine whether the annual TSR exceeds the cost of capital. In the case of Sandvik, this has not been the case for the period ranging from 2011 to 2022. It falls short by roughly 1–1.5% points in annual TSR terms, partly due to profitability being below expectations. In the first part of the period, the company struggled with its margins, and the market responded by trading the stock at a lower multiple (Fig. 14.1).

However, something occurred in the middle of the period. The business cycle took a turn for the better and simultaneously a new CEO arrived and several changes were made to its business model. The transformation involved a review of the production footprint and a shift towards a more asset-light assembly-style business model with a higher proportion of aftermarket sales. The new flexible cost structure not only resulted in more stable margins but also in a lower asset base, leading to a higher ROIC.

As we learned in the chapter about earnings quality, a low margin volatility is positively correlated not only with a stable ROIC but also with a low cost of capital. In the second part of the period, the market is regaining confidence in the company, and as a result, its valuation multiple is slowly starting to recover. Thanks to these driving forces, the annual TSR for the latter period (2016–2022) improved significantly and reached a yearly average of 17%.

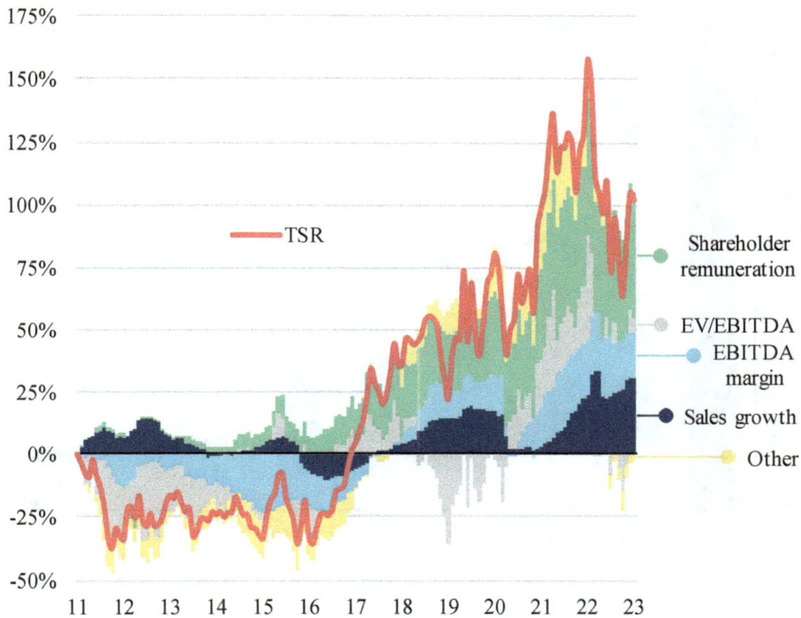

Fig. 14.1 Sandvik TSR decomposition (Dec 2010–Dec 2022)

What do the Capital Allocation Priorities and Historical Cash Flow Deployment Look Like?

Financial targets

As we discussed in the previous chapter, financial targets are essential for a company's value creation process, serving as both an internal and external guide for cash flow deployment. During the review period, Sandvik placed a strong emphasis on growth and currently aims to achieve an annual growth rate of 7%, with a focus on organic growth. The company's goal is to maintain an EBITA margin between 20% and 22%, which would result in a ROIC excluding goodwill of around 20%. Additionally, the company has set its target dividend pay-out ratio at 50%. With a conservative capital structure target, there is potential for significant acquisition activity over time (Fig. 14.2).

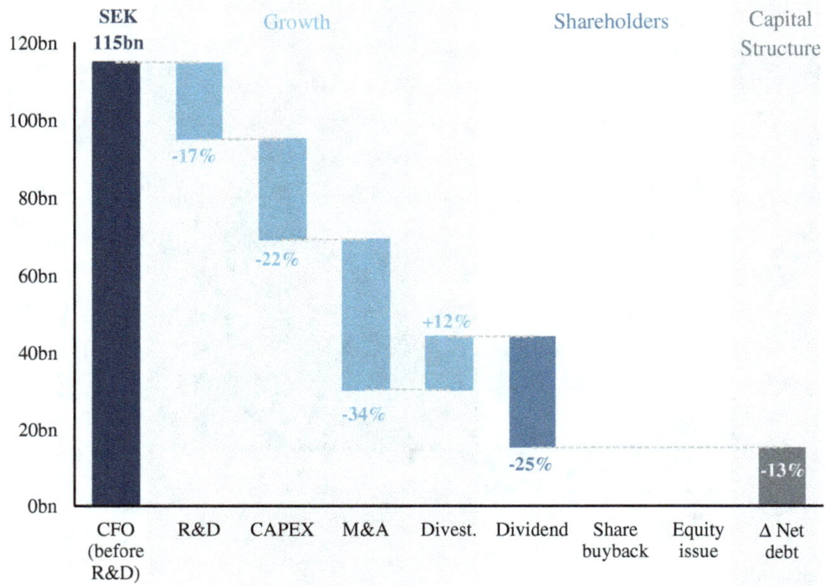

Fig. 14.2 Sandvik's cash flow deployment (2015–2021)

Cash Flow Deployment

Zooming in on the second period from 2015 to 2021, the cash flow deployment analysis reveals that 39% of CFO was utilized for organic growth investments, such as R&D and capex, while net acquisitions accounted for 22%. It is important to note that M&A-activity is not always solely focused on increasing growth; they can also aim to improve earnings quality. Sandvik's strategy exemplifies this approach, with a significant portion of its acquisitions being technology-related, aimed at transforming its business model towards a higher share of aftermarket sales. This approach has resulted in an annual growth rate of 4%, with approximately 1% attributed to currency depreciation. Given that a substantial amount of cash flow was allocated towards growth, the 4% growth rate is relatively low compared to what could have been expected.

Is the cash flow deployment, then, aligned with value creation? While a significant share of capital was allocated towards growth with a relatively meagre result, the picture is more complex considering the company's transformational journey. A large part of the investments have been made in order to lift the ROIC and earnings quality. And these investments have, as the TSR graph for the latter period confirms, been well received by the market.

Peer Comparison

How does the company fare against its peers, and what accounts for the differences between them? Does this gap analysis imply any action points for the Company?

By putting Sandvik in a peer context, we can gain some perspective on the case. The three divisions within Sandvik operate in different industries with their own distinct characteristics and competitors. The best-performing peer company produced ROIC levels above 20% during the period coupled with high organic growth numbers. This peer company managed to grow by a remarkable 8% annually by using only one-third of its cash flow from operations. The high ROIC, and the strong cash flow that followed, enabled the company to return almost two-thirds of its cash flow to the shareholders.

On the other hand, when we compare Sandvik's least profitable division to its peers, the numbers suggest a sector with more intense competitive pressure. Both the ROIC levels and the margin stability are lower in this sector. When evaluating Sandvik's three divisions alongside their respective peers, the difference in profitability and earnings quality turns out to be relatively modest.

What are the Current Market Expectations Embedded in the Valuation Multiple?

The next step in our analysis involves taking a closer look at the valuation multiples and the three attached value drivers. And as became apparent above, this must be done in a business unit context.

Sandvik's three divisions and their peers display a very diverse set of value characteristics. We now try to figure out what is priced into the company valuation multiple in terms of ROIC, growth, and cost of capital. We will start by assessing the ROIC, based partly on historical numbers (typically excluding goodwill) and partly on an assessment of the competitive landscape. There are considerable differences between the three different business units and their respective sectors. For example,

Sandvik's best performing business unit reaches a ROIC around 20%, whereas the least profitable unit displays levels around 14%.

When it comes to the growth expectations, a more homogeneous picture is often warranted—high growth rates tend to decline (revert to the mean) faster than the ROIC. We base our assessment of the third value driver, the cost of capital, on the margin volatility ratio, described in Chapter 4. There is a strong correlation between cost of capital and the profitability level of each of the three business units, which this far into the book probably does not come as a surprise.

We now calculate the warranted theoretical multiples for Sandvik and its peers and compare them with the observed market multiples. See Fig. 14.3.

The multiple for Sandvik is a weighted average of the business units. The correlations, except for Sandvik, are very high, and thus the market

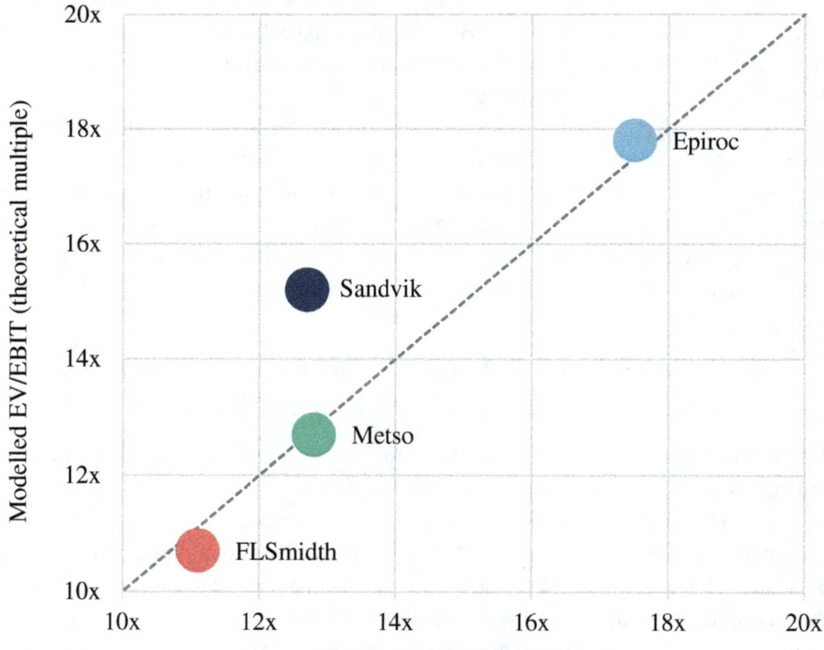

Fig. 14.3 Modelled EV/EBIT Versus Market Observed EV/EBIT

expectations for the value drivers will most likely resemble our assessments. However, the reason for Sandvik trading at a significant discount to its "fundamental" value can be explained by four potential factors:

1. The market is indicating that Sandvik bears the "burden of proof" to demonstrate confidence in its revised business model and its presumed higher earnings quality, which may require testing in more challenging market conditions. Building market confidence can often take a significant amount of time, as demonstrated by the Coloplast and Nolato case studies.
2. Even if Sandvik were to establish market confidence in its revised business model, the significant difference in the cost of capital between its business areas presents a challenge for the market to accurately assess the company's overall cost of capital.
3. While the market shows increasing confidence in senior management's ability to allocate capital, there are still concerns about engaging in expensive M&A activity. Large and expensive M&As could potentially result in the stock underperforming, as investors might question whether the deal would generate value for shareholders.
4. Similarly, it will be essential to avoid suboptimal allocation of capital among business units to maintain investor confidence in the long run. Many companies tend to allocate capital based on factors such as growth prospects, operating margins, market position, and past cash flow deployment. However, none of these factors alone are true drivers of value. If the correlation between these factors and the realized return on invested capital, growth, and earnings quality is low, the company is exposed to the risk of suboptimal capital allocation.

What Does an "Optimal" Capital Structure Look Like Given the Capital Allocation Priorities?

Given Sandvik's high growth ambitions, positive market outlook, and strong profitability, it would be prudent for the company to strive for a capital structure that offers high funding flexibility and robust liquidity back-up. This is manifested by considering Sandvik's A-rating from Standard & Poor's, conservative financial leverage target (net debt/EBITDA of 1.5×), and strong liquidity back-up.

How Can the Capital Allocation and Financial Targets Be Communicated to the Market?

We could summarize the business case from a market perspective as follows:

1. **Transformation case**
   The operational improvements have been successful and the valuation is now at a crossroads. Long-term organic growth prospects have become the primary value driver. The executed spin-off was not significant enough in size in order to result in a full revaluation of the company.
2. **Capital allocation**
   Capital allocation priorities between operations are in focus longer term, as the business units display different opportunities for value creation. Moreover, growth strategies based on acquisitions are hard to evaluate for investors but key for capital allocation and value creation.
3. **Valuation potential not yet reached**
   The company's share price has not yet reached its "theoretical" potential. Therefore, if a major acquisition takes place, new equity may be viewed as relatively expensive for current owners, risking an unnecessarily high dilution. As such, it is unlikely to be the preferred method of payment.
4. **Re-valuation trigger—earnings quality confirmation**
   If the company can handle the next downturn with higher margin stability, it is likely that the cost of capital will decrease, significantly impacting valuation.
5. **More room for action**
   If none of the above triggers a revaluation of the Sandvik stock, further spin-offs can be expected in the long term. Additionally, a revision of how to use the balance sheet to create value for shareholders is possible.

Based on our market-based assessment of Sandvik and its drivers of value creation, we have three questions to pose:

Are the Communicated Targets in Line with the Market's Views of Value Creation?

First and foremost, we can conclude that Sandvik's four goals effectively cover a large portion of the value drivers. While growth is prioritized, it's important to note that there's a significant difference between organic and acquired growth when it comes to value creation. Sandvik addresses this by differentiating its growth targets into organic and acquired growth.

When it comes to the margin target (EBITA margin of 20–22%), it translates into a ROIC of around 17–18% (including goodwill), which is well above the cost of capital. Additionally, the margin target is expressed as a range, which highlights the importance of having a flexible cost base and a high earnings quality. This ultimately has the potential to translate into a lower cost of capital.

The target for the capital structure, which states that the net debt to EBITDA should be 1.5 times, indicates that leverage is not considered a priority for value creation. This is consistent with the prevailing market view.

The dividend target, which aims at a 50% pay-out ratio, could be seen as a shareholder-friendly ambition, but its success ultimately depends on Sandvik's cash flow generation.

However, as the three business units have their own unique characteristics, the priority of the value drivers will differ. It is unclear to us whether all three business units are governed by the same set of targets. If so, the conglomerate discount may very well be warranted.

Are the Targets Consistent with Each Other?

In order to find out whether the dividend target could be in interference with the high growth ambition, we use the formula described in the previous chapter. Assuming a ROIC of 17%, a growth target of 7% would result in a break-even dividend pay-out of 63%, indicating some margin for achieving the target. However, if the growth were to be driven by acquisitions with a much lower ROIC, the outcome would change significantly.

Priority of Targets

A clear financial target and capital allocation prioritization send signals both internally and externally about the focus and importance of the different goals. Sandvik faces the challenge of striking a balance between its growth ambitions, margin targets, and the market's high appreciation of earnings quality. While it is understandable that Sandvik may struggle to prioritize these goals, it will need the skillset to determine which lever to pull when prioritizing these value-drivers in the future. Sandvik also faces the challenge to adopt tailor-made prioritizations for each business unit individually.

Only time will tell whether the market is correctly pricing Sandvik with a discount to its fundamental value, or if Sandvik will ultimately prove to be a good enough capital allocator in order to erase the conglomerate discount.

CHAPTER 15

A Three-Step Capital Allocation Framework

The CEO's main objective is to maximize the long-term value per share. This book has demonstrated that total shareholder return does not necessarily correlate with growth, nor does it correlate with any other capital allocation activity on an overall level. Therefore, each CEO must determine the optimal course of action for their company based on its unique circumstances. While there is no one-size-fits-all solution, a thorough understanding of the value creation framework is an essential starting point for developing effective capital allocation strategies.

Drawing on a combination of in-depth research, empirical studies, and insights from client meetings, we have put together this book with the hope of giving corporate decision-makers valuable practical knowledge about the art of capital allocation and value creation.

We summarize the findings of this book in the form of a three-step capital allocation framework where we first will *determine the relative importance of the three value drivers*, before turning to the *evaluation of the cash flow deployment options with a "risk-reward" mind-set*. The third and last step involves *setting KPIs and financial target priorities* that are aligned with the company's value creation proposition.

T. Arenbo, *Capital Allocation and Value Creation*,
https://doi.org/10.1007/978-3-031-47048-6_15

Step 1—Determine the Relative Importance of the Three Value Drivers

The first crucial step involves identifying the relative priorities of the three value drivers. The specific strategy to adopt and the appropriate value creation lever to pull can vary greatly from one company to another, as we have frequently seen in this book.

In order to establish the correct starting point for the priorities, it is essential to examine the relationship between the ROIC and the cost of capital. By doing so, we can determine the optimal approach for each value driver. And most importantly, before focusing too much on growth as a value driver, it is crucial to first establish a solid competitive advantage and foundation in terms of the ROIC versus cost of capital spread.

Emphasis on the ROIC and the Durability of Excess Returns

ROIC is the cash flow engine of the company from which value creation originates. A high and stable ROIC is often a sign of a sustainable competitive advantage and a strong business model. In addition, a high ROIC enables the company to fund future growth with internally generated cash flows.

From a valuation perspective, the marginal benefit of focusing on profitability is very high when ROIC is close to the cost of capital, which makes it a top priority focus area for a large part of the company universe.

Whether ROIC or a similar balance-sheet based ratio, such as return on capital employed (ROCE), is used, is generally of less importance. However, decision-makers should not confuse the focus on ROIC with that of operating margins. Managers should be careful not to overlook the fact that different operations may require varying levels of capital usage, as this can have a significant impact on value creation.

While discussing operating margins, market position, and product offerings may seem intuitive, it's important to understand the true drivers behind value creation for effective capital allocation. By prioritizing ROIC, executives can make more informed decisions that account for profitability as well as capital efficiency.

There are numerous benefits to be gained from prioritizing profitability as a crucial aspect of business operations. For instance, a company's ROIC level is often positively correlated with both its earnings quality and growth rates. Although higher profitability does not guarantee above-average sales within a sector, companies that can maintain a consistent above-average profitability over the long term are likely to enjoy significant competitive advantages in terms of market share and sales. This phenomenon is evident in some of the cases reviewed in this book, such as Elisa and Royal Unibrew.

Earnings Quality and Cost of Capital

Second in priority when it comes to value drivers is often the somewhat overlooked aspect of earnings quality. As stated above, earnings quality frequently correlates with the return on invested capital, making it difficult to analyze in isolation. Despite these limitations, we are confident that strategies linked to improved earnings quality can have a significant positive impact on a firm's valuation. We also think it is fair to claim that, for too many companies, earnings quality as a value driver has not received the strategic focus it deserves.

Earnings quality is a crucial element in valuation, primarily due to its close connection with the cost of capital. Although it may take some time for the market to acknowledge improvements in earnings quality, once it does, every future dollar earned by the company will appreciate in value. For instance, reducing the cost of capital by one percentage point can potentially result in a 15–20% increase in the firm's value. The case studies of Nolato and Coloplast offer examples of successfully implemented strategies that have enhanced earnings quality and lowered the cost of capital.

We believe that in many industries, particularly the more mature ones, business strategies that prioritize improving earnings quality are more likely to generate greater value than strategies focused solely on growth. Again, this is due to the strong link between earnings quality and cost of capital, a connection that may be overlooked if management is overly fixated on growth or margin expansion. While these are worthy goals, pursuing them at the expense of earnings quality risks resulting in a dilution of overall value. Therefore, it's important for businesses to balance their growth ambitions with a focus on maintaining high-quality earnings.

Inflationary environments, such as the post-pandemic period, further highlight the significance of earnings quality and pricing power.

Growth—A Double-Edged Sword

As emphasized in our study of total shareholder return in Chapter 3, the top performers in our sample were dominated by high-growth companies. Undoubtedly, growth plays an essential role in creating value, and it has been in very high demand among investors in the low-growth environment we have experienced since the global financial crisis. Nevertheless, it's important to recognize that growth can be a double-edged sword, as it is a very strong driver of value creation for a relatively limited number of companies. It is important to keep in mind that pursuing strategies targeted towards growth tend to come with a higher risk to shareholder return.

Therefore, successful companies often try to adopt a low-risk strategy to approach growth by focusing on developing competitive advantages and achieving above-average profitability. This approach often results in higher-than-average sector growth, as companies with higher profitability have greater financial resources to invest in areas such as research and development, marketing and other growth initiatives. These investments can help them gain a larger market share and expand into new markets without diluting profitability. We believe that this has been an important strategy to drive organic growth for several top-performing companies that we reviewed, such as Atlas Copco and Novo Nordisk.

Among the less successful companies striving for growth, a common denominator turns out to be acquiring high-growth companies in order to compensate for a slow-growing and competitive core market. However, the strategic differences between slow and high growth companies, such as cost focus, innovation and culture, make integration and capital allocation challenging. This strategy has cost dearly in terms of severely underperforming TSR for companies like Ericsson, Telia and Sanoma, just to mention a few.

Step 2—Evaluating Cash Flow Deployment Options With a "Risk-Reward" Mind-Set

Once a company has determined its approach to balancing the three value drivers, it opens up for a multitude of cash flow deployment strategies. However, to make informed decisions when evaluating these options, it's essential for management to embrace a "risk-reward" mind-set.

When it comes to thinking in a "risk-reward" mind-set, we believe corporate executives can learn from the way many investors approach the subject. Figure 15.1 is a stylized attempt to illustrate how the equity market might view a company's expected value creation across different cash flow deployment options, taking into account the associated risks.[1]

Cash flow deployment options with positive expected risk-adjusted values are positioned above the line, while those with negative expected risk-adjusted values are below it. In this particular example, which we believe is representative for a relatively large part of the firm universe, maintenance capex is depicted as having the most favourable risk/reward ratio, whereas large acquisitions have the lowest probability of being value creative.

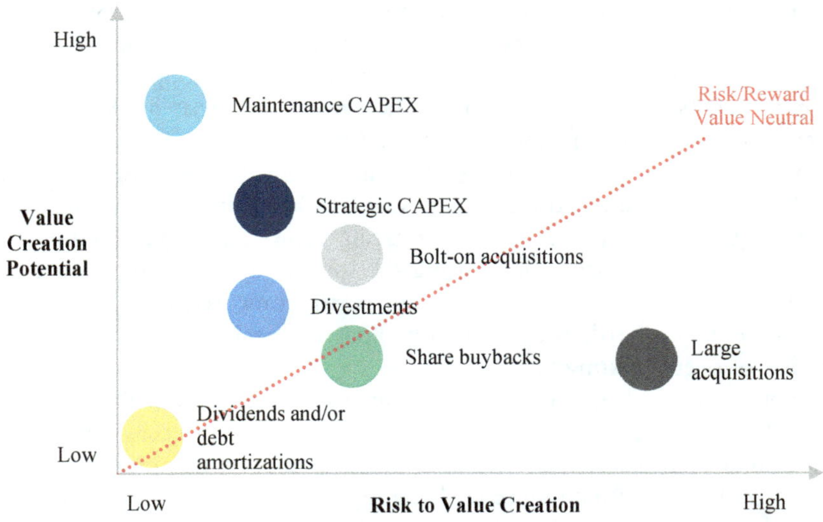

Fig. 15.1 Capital allocation in a risk-reward perspective

[1] The picture above depicts a plausible outcome given a company with a moderately positive ROIC spread, reasonable growth prospect, and a balanced capital structure. The expected value of the various cash flow deployment alternatives will change depending on the conditions for value creation. For instance, a company with a low ROIC spread acting in mature markets would see a higher value of returning capital to owners rather than reinvesting any available cash flow. Thus, in such a case, the capex would be closer to the value neutral line.

To provide further insight into the risk/return profiles of different capital deployment options, we present a brief summary below where we highlight key considerations for each option as well as try to pinpoint some "value pitfalls" related to each deployment alternative.

Maintenance and Strategic Investments

If we include all investments that drive organic growth, i.e. maintenance and strategic capex as well as R&D and other internal spending that creates tangible and intangible assets, these constitute the largest share of the capital that companies allocate (CAPEX alone stood for 36% of net cash flow from operations in the Nordics during the ten year period ending in 2022).

It starts with the **bare-bones maintenance capex**, which can be viewed as a necessity in order to keep the "license to operate". In most companies, decisions around bare-bones investments pass through investment committees smoothly. However, if the return on these investments is lower than the cost of capital, it may be more prudent to accept a loss in market share rather than invest in maintenance at a low rate of return.

When we move to **strategic capex**, it can be defined as the expenditure required for the purpose of facilitating growth, but in a sense it can be viewed as a necessity for securing the long-term license to operate as well. Strategic capex comes with a higher risk compared to maintenance investments. One risk associated with allocating capital to strategic capex is that of over-investing.

For instance, value erosion may take place when companies attempt to achieve growth in stagnating sectors at too high a cost. While this error may appear straightforward to avoid in theory, historical evidence indicates that it is much more challenging to avoid in real life. A particularly delicate situation takes place in competitive, low-profitability sectors, when companies evaluate large capex programmes that on paper may have high expected returns. However, competitors will likely respond to the company's investment plans, which eventually will bring profitability down to levels close to, or even below, the cost of capital. In this kind of competitive sectors, companies must constantly run just to stay in place.

Considering the inherent risks associated with growth strategies, it is not uncommon for companies to reinvest their capital, either organically or through acquisitions, at rates that are below their cost of capital. It is important to note that poor returns on an investment may not necessarily be attributed to poor management decisions. Rather, a risk-reward framework operates on probabilities; and some investments with a positive expected return may still result in poor realized returns due to factors such as unfortunate market timing or simply bad luck.

A combined risk and reward framework for evaluating investments highlights the importance for companies to think of capital allocation in terms of "strategies" rather than "projects". Strategies can be seen as a portfolio of projects where some will not pay off even though the strategy as a whole is value creating.

Acquired Growth—Comes With a Higher Risk to TSR

When we move further down the "risk/reward ladder" we come to the various kinds of inorganic growth options. M&As are one of the biggest cash spends for corporates and almost on a par in size with that of the organic cash spend (29% of net CFO). Despite its widespread popularity, acquiring companies generally struggle to reach positive returns from takeover deals. However, the expected returns vary greatly between the different types of M&As. This suggests that executives at acquiring companies should put in extra effort to master the art of deal-making.

The top-ranked type of acquisition when it comes to "deal success probability" is those where serial acquirers buy privately owned companies. They typically have a *long-term acquisition strategy*, a *deep understanding of their sector*, and focus their acquisitions on targets within the *same industry*. In some cases, the buyer has established a strong reputation as an acquirer and is considered the *preferred buyer* for *privately owned companies*. These companies also often have a decentralized organization that allows local management to benefit from the advantages of a larger parent company, such as in supply management, funding, and sales organization.

At the other end of the risk and reward scale, we find acquisitions made in order to boost growth outside a slow-growing core market. Large public acquisitions outside a company's home markets seem to be a recipe for low returns. Large acquisitions also tend to simultaneously lead to a materially higher operational as well as financial risk. In addition, there is a risk of poor market timing, as acquisition activity often coincides with booming economies and elevated corporate valuations.

When it comes to inorganic growth, it is worth noting that even though it is common for the equity market to trade down the value of a company that announces large acquisitions, this does not necessarily indicate that the market believes the acquisition has a negative expected value. Large acquisitions with negative share price reactions can also be a sign of differing preferences between the equity market and management regarding the company's overall risk level. The lower share price can thus result from the equity market increasing the risk premium and, consequently, the cost of capital for the company.

As a final remark on inorganic growth, we would like to highlight how the market can view value creation of inorganic versus organic growth and how it can become visible in the multiple. When we compare the two global industrial companies Assa Abloy and Atlas Copco, the former trades around 14× EV/EBITA while the latter trades around 18×. Why is Atlas Copco trading so much higher when the fundamental value drivers like earnings quality and goodwill adjusted ROIC are relatively similar? Even for the third value driver, the growth rate, there are great similarities, as both companies have had a CAGR of nearly 10% during the last 10 years. However, for Atlas Copco a majority of that growth has been organically generated, whereas for Assa Abloy it has been a mix of organic and inorganic growth. A large part of the valuation difference can thus be attributed to how the companies are expected to grow and at what costs.

Why Less So Often Is More

There is no denying that divestitures, overall, have generated value for shareholders, even though evidence suggests a wide range of results. Our peer study in Chapter 6 highlights the importance of the balance between reduced agency costs and increased strategic flexibility, on one side, and the potential loss of value stemming from potential dis-synergies, on the other. Successful spin-offs, for instance, are more prevalent in fragmented and emerging industries, whereas the opposite holds true for mature sectors like utilities and consumer staples.

A TSR analysis of the successful spin-offs gives a clear indication of what drivers to look for in a potential demerger. Given that the multiple expansion ranks very high among the performance drivers, it seems that releasing the conglomerate discount and finding the right investor base is a top priority. The second most important driver is the sales increase, which highlights how important it is to find the right organizational structure for a business strategy aiming at growth. But we can also conclude that not all business units are better off being on their own. In some cases, the dis-synergies are too big and the new company is too small to be a stand-alone entity. In these cases, a trade-sale might be the preferred route to follow.

Returning Excess Cash

Returning cash to shareholders accounts for approximately 30% of net cash flow from operations and involves in most cases a significantly lower risk to value creation than the other allocation alternatives. From a purely theoretical standpoint, pay-outs to shareholders, at least in the form of dividends, are value neutral as they do not increase the cash flow to the firm. Nevertheless, the findings presented in this book suggest that the equity market places considerable emphasis on management returning excess cash to shareholders. One of the most common capital allocation errors is, as previously highlighted, no doubt when companies with strong free cash flow, low debt levels, and operations in mature markets pursue growth strategies at an excessively high cost. This example underscores how decisions regarding pay-out policies can be linked to discussions surrounding the capital structure.

Share buybacks offer a riskier alternative to dividends for companies seeking to return cash to shareholders. The "Buffet approach" where share buybacks are not merely a method of returning surplus cash to shareholders, but a potential investment opportunity, adds a new level of expertise required for a corporate capital allocator. In order to qualify as prioritized cash deployment usage, the stock should be valued below its so-called intrinsic value. This means that corporate management must be able to distinguish between price and value. Only the most skilled investors have the confidence to adopt this seldom deployed approach to capital allocation.

Moreover, share buybacks tend to display a pro-cyclical pattern which means that companies buy back more shares when their stock is expensive. This poses a big risk to the potential "return" the share buybacks will yield for the investors that a company should preferably care about, namely those who remain owners of the company.

However, a SBB mandate can form an important part of a pay-out policy that mitigates the risk of value-diluting growth strategies. This is to ensure that major acquisitions and investments are always evaluated against the option of repurchasing the companies' own shares.

Capital Structure

Now we turn our attention to the role of capital structure in the value creation process. For most companies, we believe that the potential costs of excessive leverage outweigh the costs of underleveraging. Given that economic and financial tail risks cannot be precisely anticipated in likelihood and magnitude, leverage should in most cases err on the side of caution. For instance, companies with a positive ROIC spread and reasonable growth prospects should focus on managing the capital structure for *financial flexibility*, which includes keeping leverage relatively low. This group should aim to maintain a flexible capital structure that provides room for manoeuvring and helps them take advantage of growth opportunities as they arise.

On the other hand, for companies with a lower and more volatile ROIC, the decision regarding capital structure should be influenced by the risk and potential cost of *financial distress*. For such companies, the mismanagement of the liability side of the balance sheet can lead to value destruction. Thus, it is essential to focus on maintaining a sound capital structure that can withstand potential stress scenarios.

However, for a third group of companies, those with stable ROIC and low-growth prospects, the capital structure becomes a tool for value creation. These companies, typically found in sectors such as telecom and real estate, can benefit from leverage, which not only reduces the cost of capital but also helps prevent management from overinvesting in low-growth markets.

Step 3—A Practical Guide to Capital Allocation Priorities

At this stage of the process, we are hopefully able to confidently answer the question: "What are the value driver priorities for the company?" We have also gained a better understanding of the cash flow deployment alternatives and the different "risk-reward" characteristics attached to them. In the third and last step of our capital allocation framework, it is time to include the owners' risk preferences as a piece of the puzzle. After a brief discussion about the importance of incorporating the investors' perspective, we summarize the framework focusing on financial targets and their priorities.

As executives manage assets on behalf of the owners, it is crucial that their actions align with the investors' objectives. Therefore, management must ensure that the *level of risk* with which they choose to run the company aligns with the investors' risk tolerance. That also includes taking the "right" kind of risks to generate the highest possible risk-reward outcome.

Thus, a well-designed capital allocation framework should include financial targets and incentive programmes that serve to *reduce agency costs* and mitigate the risk of the market losing trust in management's *capital allocation capabilities*. To address potential agency costs, it is worth highlighting the set of guiding principles followed by CEOs at Berkshire Hathaway when running their businesses. These principles involve running the company as if they were the sole owner, managing it as their sole asset, and committing never to sell or merge it for a period of 50 years. See page 7 Cunningham (2013).

Adopting an owner or investor mind-set can significantly reduce the agency costs resulting from common managerial missteps discussed in this book. One recurring theme, for instance, is that managers often underestimate the requirements of being the "best owner" of a company or business unit. Additionally, this book provides perspective on the sometimes substantial challenges associated with managing businesses that have diverse strategies and cultures. Adopting an investor mind-set encourages a disciplined and rational approach to decision-making, as well as a thorough analysis of risks and opportunities, which can contribute to mitigating behavioural challenges associated with ownership and management.

Financial Target Priorities Aligned With Long-Term Value Creation

Optimal capital allocation priorities vary depending on specific circumstances, so there is no one-size-fits-all answer. However, we firmly believe that a comprehensive understanding of the factors influencing competitive advantage and profitability is the natural starting point for any analysis aimed at creating value. In Fig. 15.2, we attempt to illustrate some fundamental capital allocation priorities for a set of "stylized" positions governed by the ROIC versus cost of capital spread, or as Buffet might have put it, the size of the "protective moats".

The valuation multiple, when used wisely and with some caution, can provide valuable insights to the management and board, as it indirectly can serve as a second opinion about appropriate capital allocation priorities. The priorities provided in Fig. 15.2 are rough guides only, and should by no means prevent a company from exploring alternative strategies. However, if the chosen capital allocation strategy deviates from the suggested "recommendations", some extra consideration and thorough justification may be called for. After all, capital allocation mistakes can be very costly, and few executives possess the capital allocation skills of Warren Buffet and the other "outsiders" mentioned by Thorndike. If our Nordic sample group had adhered to the guiding priorities, many value-destroying allocation decisions could certainly have been avoided, saving shareholders a lot of money.

1. Turnaround or Restructuring Focus

Multiples: EV/EBITA multiples below 8–9× might indicate difficulties in reaching sufficient profitability to create value. The price-to-book ratio might also be worth having a look at as values below 1× can be an indicator that the company struggles to meet the "one-dollar-test".

Description of company situation: A challenged business model.

Operational and strategic focus on cutting costs and improving the operating cash flow. Increasing emphasis on the core business by shrinking the company through, for example, asset divestments. The latter, combined with new equity and streamlined working capital, facilitates the important task of strengthening the balance sheet.

The most important **TSR drivers** include increased margins and reduced leverage. As a consequence, the prioritized **financial targets** are margin and balance sheet targets.

2. ROIC and Earnings Quality Focus

Companies in our second group often display **EV/EBITA-Multiples** around 9–13×.

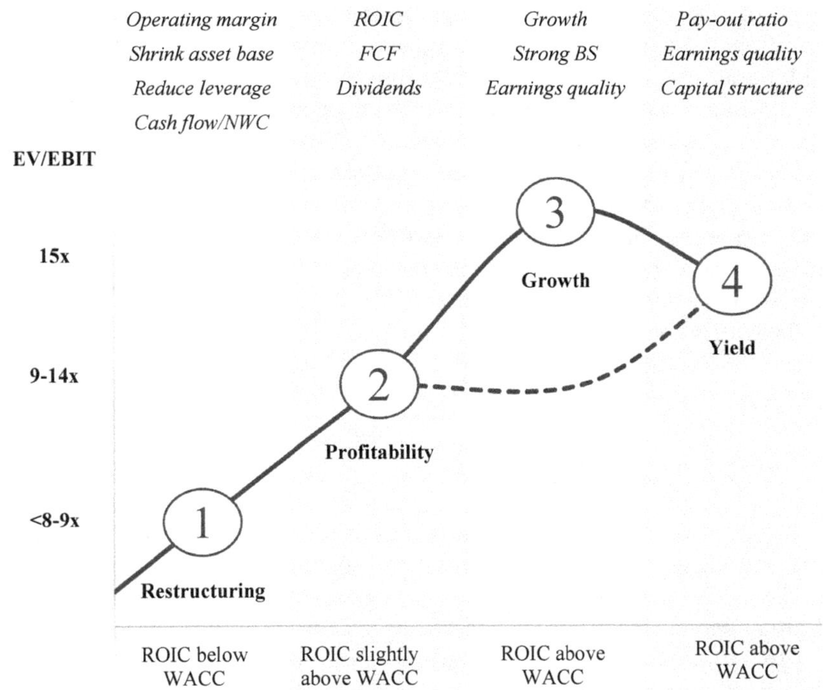

Fig. 15.2 Capital aligning the value creation proposition with the financial targets

Description of company situation: Companies in this group have viable business models but the competitive landscape limits the profitability to levels close to the cost of capital. These are companies that typically "need to do a lot of running just to keep in the same place".

Operational and strategic focus should primarily be targeted towards improving ROIC with, for instance, differentiation or cost leadership strategies. Additionally, the marginal value of improving earnings quality can be high. This can be achieved through, for instance, implementing measures to improve cost flexibility or pricing power. At the same time, firms in this competitive environment need to pay close attention to the levels of investment, carefully weighing the risk of under—as well as over-investing. Increased sales that come at the expense of a margin dilution and higher earnings volatility would most likely be value destructive.

Suitable **financial targets:** Prioritize operating margins and asset utilization and keep a close eye on the ROIC versus cost of capital spread. Balance sheet targets could be set as a range, leaning to the conservative side. To help ensure that management allocates capital in a disciplined way, it is important to set a dividend policy that signals a high opportunity cost for the free cash flow generated by the company. Growth targets should normally have a low priority.

TSR drivers: Increased ROIC and shareholder remuneration.

3. Growth Focus

In this group of companies, we find the highest **multiples** which can reach levels around 15–40×.

Description of company situation: Firms in this category are active in growing markets or know how to expand their product offerings into new markets. They successfully pursue a cost leadership and/or differentiation strategy generating a strong ROIC versus cost of capital spread.

Operational and strategic focus should put a very clear emphasis on growth. For most companies in this group, it is sufficient to keep ROIC and margins at stable levels. Improving margins at the expense of a lower growth rate would likely be value dilutive.

Financial targets: Prioritize growth and set long-term targets, preferably with specified organic and inorganic contributions. Balance sheet targets should be set conservatively in order to preserve financial flexibility. Margin and dividend targets may be given lower priority.

TSR drivers: Growth (and to some extent multiple expansion).

4. Earnings Quality and Yield

Multiples: EV/EBITA multiples of 15–25×.

Description of company situation: Companies in this group are characterized by having a very high-earnings quality and, consequently, low cost of capital.

Operational and strategic focus: These companies are active in stable and slow-growing markets and often have market-leading positions with strong competitive advantages.

In this group, it is common to set **financial targets** that include a very high pay-out ratio as well as a low-growth target. As the cost of capital is key for a high valuation, it is important not to jeopardize the earnings quality by setting too aggressive margin or sales targets. Balance sheet targets can often be set at a considerably higher level for this category of companies compared to the other three groups.

TSR drivers: Shareholder remuneration activity including dividends and share buybacks potentially coupled with multiple expansion (lower cost of capital).

The market-based capital allocation framework presented in this book serves as a starting point for understanding the subject. It aims to offer valuable insights and perspectives, and the framework should be viewed as a practical tool and a source of inspiration. This framework can hopefully provide a structured approach for management, boards, and other stakeholders to consider capital allocation decisions and strategies. And maybe most importantly, it encourages critical thinking and informed decision-making, when executives try to excel in the art of capital allocation.

Reference

Cunningham LA (2013) The Essays of Warren Buffet—Lessons for Corporate America. Carolina Academic Press, Third edition (p. 205ff)

Appendix 1: Evaluating Management's Capital Allocation Skills

It is not always easy to distinguish between skill and luck when evaluating management's capital allocation success. Below, we provide a list of questions that can help to shed some light on this important but challenging issue.

Explaining the business strategy

- Is the business strategy easy to understand when explained by the management?
- Is management answering questions clearly and precisely?

TSR decomposition

- What have been the main sources of shareholder return?
- Are they in line with the business strategy?

Past cash flow deployment

- What does the historical pattern look like? Have there been significant changes, or has cash flow deployment been stable over time?
- How does it compare to peers?
- Are the cash flow deployment activities coherent with the company's value creation proposition?

T. Arenbo, *Capital Allocation and Value Creation*,
https://doi.org/10.1007/978-3-031-47048-6

Profitability

- Examine the ROIC over time and compare it to peers, both including and excluding goodwill.
- What are the sources of ROIC (for example consumer or production advantages), and are they in line with expectations given the business strategy?

Choice of risk level for management

- Does management fully understand the concept of risk and reward? And do they know how to determine an "appropriate" overall level of risk?
- If the company has a growth agenda, is it primarily based on organic or inorganic initiatives?
- Is the financial risk level appropriate for the business strategy and ownership composition?

Financial Targets

- Are the financial targets in line with the value creation proposition?
- Are the financial targets internally consistent with each other?

Management incentives

- How much stock do senior management and board members own?
- Is the incentive structure aligned with the value creation proposition and long-term owners' risk preferences?
- What kind of relationship/discussions does management have with its long-term shareholders?

Management's understanding of capital allocation and value creation. Can management, for example, answer questions like:

- What is the cost of capital for the company?
- What are the market expectations embedded in the share price?
- Is the company priced in line with its intrinsic value?
- Why is the company the best owner of Division X or Company Y?

Accounting standards

- Is management transparent and prudent in its approach to accounting?

Appendix 2: A Business Strategy Summary

A business strategy defines the company's target market, competitive positioning, and overall direction. A well-crafted and executed business strategy can help a company achieve sustainable competitive advantages and long-term growth, while a poorly executed one can lead to stagnation or decline. Below we list some of the most commonly used strategies.

A **cost leadership strategy** involves a company aiming to be the low-cost producer in its industry. This can be achieved through economies of scale, efficient operations, and tight cost control. Companies that employ this strategy aim to offer products or services at lower prices than their competitors while still maintaining a reasonable profit margin.

A **differentiation strategy** involves a company creating unique and superior products or services that command a premium price. This can be achieved through product innovation, brand building, and superior customer service. Companies that employ this strategy aim to create a unique value proposition that sets them apart from their competitors. The success of this strategy is often tied to a company's ability to maintain a competitive advantage in differentiation through product innovation and brand building.

A **market niche strategy** involves a company targeting a specific segment of the market with specialized products or services. This can be achieved by identifying a specific market segment that is underserved, or by creating a unique value proposition that appeals to a specific group of

T. Arenbo, *Capital Allocation and Value Creation*,
https://doi.org/10.1007/978-3-031-47048-6

customers. The success of this strategy is often tied to a company's ability to maintain a competitive advantage in the niche market.

Diversification strategy involves a company expanding its operations into new markets or new products or services. This can be achieved through acquisitions, joint ventures, or internal development. Companies that employ this strategy aim to reduce risk by spreading their operations across multiple markets or products.

A **Blue Ocean strategy** is a business strategy that involves creating a new market space that is uncontested by existing competitors. This can be achieved by identifying untapped market opportunities, creating new products or services, or by targeting new customer segments. The success of this strategy is often tied to a company's ability to create a new market space through unique and innovative business models.

When ranking these strategies, it is important to note that each strategy has its own set of advantages and disadvantages, and the success of a strategy will depend on the specific circumstances of the company and its industry. However, in general, a cost leadership strategy tends to have a lower success rate compared to differentiation and market niche strategies, as it can be difficult for companies to maintain a cost advantage in the long term. Blue Ocean strategies, while having a high potential for success, also have a higher level of risk and uncertainty. As was highlighted in Chapter 6, diversification as a strategy is inherently difficult and requires management to be skilled capital allocators as well as business strategists, and the culture to be consistent throughout the entire organization.

Appendix 3: ROIC Calculation Extended

When calculating ROIC, adjustments to the numerator and denominator often have to be made. ROIC should reflect the operating performance of a company, so it's important to exclude non-operating items such as non-recurring gains or losses. Some companies may have significant off-balance sheet items such as operating leases, pension obligations, or contingent liabilities. It's important to assess whether and how these items should be included in the calculation of invested capital. Some other common and influential adjustments include non-operating and non-cash taxes in the income tax provision, treatment of write-offs, and deferred equity compensation liabilities.

How to Think About Intangible Assets and the Use of ROIC

Another important factor to take into consideration when calculating ROIC is the treatment and potential adjustments of intangible assets like capitalized R&D. Here are some key considerations:

NOPAT: By using EBITA, and not EBIT, as the starting point for calculating NOPAT, a more accurate picture of a company's profitability can be obtained. However, it is important to deduct any amortization of intangible assets that have been capitalized, i.e. those that accounting-wise are treated similarly to the depreciation of capital expenditures. If the "A" in EBITA for example represents amortization of acquired intangible assets, it should normally be a part of the NOPAT. This is so since the

T. Arenbo, *Capital Allocation and Value Creation*,
https://doi.org/10.1007/978-3-031-47048-6

company is probably including these "investments" in the cost of goods sold. Deducting the amortization of these kinds of acquired intangibles risks double-counting the costs.

Invested capital: When calculating invested capital, it is important to be aware of how the value of intangible assets is treated accounting-wise. After all, they can represent a meaningful share of the company's investment in its business. Only the value of the *capitalized* intangible assets will show up on a company's balance sheet. Those R&D costs that are expensed, which is the vast majority, will not create an intangible asset on the balance sheet. Thus, companies that invest heavily in intangible assets will accounting-wise have a lower level of assets on the balance sheet than companies with a larger share of traditional capex. Adjusting for this accounting anomaly would normally result in a less extreme ROIC distribution for companies expensing their intangible investments.

When comparing the ROIC of companies within the same industry, it is important to consider differences in the amount and type of intangible assets and capitalized R&D. Companies vary in their approach to capitalizing R&D, which may lead to different levels of invested capital, and thus could impact their ROIC. For an in-depth analysis of how to calculate ROIC and how to handle common issues, we recommend reading Mauboussin and Callahan (2022).

References

Chapter 1

Buffet WE (1987) Letter to Shareholders. Berkshire Hathaway Annual Report.

Graham JR, Harvey CR, Puri M (2013) Managerial Attitudes and Corporate Actions. Journal of Financial Economics 109: 103–121.

Steven N, Kaplan SN, Sorensen M (2020) Are CFOs Different? Published Online. https://papers.ssrn.com/sol3/papers.cfm?abstract_id=2747691.

Thorndike WN (2012) The Outsiders: Eight Unconventional CEOs and Their Radically Rational Blueprint for Success. Harvard Business School Publishing.

Chapter 2

Chancellor E (2015) Capital Returns: Investing Through the Capital Cycle—A Money Manager's Reports 2002–2015. Palgrave Macmillan.

Chung KH, Wright P, Charoenwong C (1998) Investment Opportunities and Market Reaction to Capital Expenditure Decisions. Journal of Banking & Finance 22(1): 41–60.

Damodaran (2023) Damodaran Online. https://pages.stern.nyu.edu/~adamodar/. Accessed 15 March 2023.

ECB (2018) Measuring and Interpreting the Cost of Equity in the Euro Area. Published Online. https://www.ecb.europa.eu/pub/economic-bulletin/articles/2018/html/ecb.ebart201804_02.en.html.

Graham JR (2022) Presidential Address: Corporate Finance and Reality. Journal of Finance 77(4): 1975–2049.

T. Arenbo, *Capital Allocation and Value Creation*,
https://doi.org/10.1007/978-3-031-47048-6

Magretta J (2012) Understanding Michael Porter—The Essential Guide to Competition and Strategy. Harvard Business Review Press.

McConnell JJ, Muscarella CJ (1985) Corporate Capital Expenditure Decisions and the Market Value of the Firm. Journal of Financial Economics 14(3): 399–422.

McKinsey (2006) Balancing ROIC and Growth to Build Value. Published Online. https://www.mckinsey.com/capabilities/strategy-and-corporate-finance/our-insights/balancing-roic-and-growth-to-build-value.

McKinsey & Company, Koller T, Goedhart M, Wessels D (2020) Valuation: Measuring and Managing the Value of Companies. Wiley.

Porter ME (1980) Competitive Strategy. Free Press.

PwC (2022) Riskpremien på den svenska aktiemarknaden. Published Online. https://www.pwc.se/sv/corporate-finance/riskpremiestudien-2022.pdf.

Raynor ME, Ahmed M (2013) The Three Rules: How Exceptional Companies Think. Penguin Publishing Group.

Chapter 3

BCG (2015) Value Creation for the Rest of Us—The 2015 Value Creators Report. Published Online. https://web-assets.bcg.com/img-src/BCG-Value-Creation-for-the-Rest-of-Us-Jul-2015_tcm9-171215.pdf.

Chapter 4

Merton RC (1974) On the Pricing of Corporate Debt: The Risk Structure of Interest Rates. The Journal of Finance 29(2): 449–470.

Part 2

Mauboussin MJ, Callahan D (2022) Capital Allocation—Results, Analysis and Assessment. Published Online. https://www.morganstanley.com/im/publication/insights/articles/article_capitalallocation.pdf.

McKinsey (2020) Divesting with Agility. Published Online. https://www.mckinsey.com/capabilities/strategy-and-corporate-finance/our-insights/divesting-with-agility.

Chapter 5

Clark PJ, Mills RW (2013) Masterminding the Deal: Breakthroughs in M&A Strategy and Analysis, Kogan Page (Chapter 4).

Conn RL, Cosh A, Guest PM, Hughes A (2005) The Impact on UK Acquirers of Domestic, Cross-border, Public and Private Acquisitions. Journal of Business Finance & Accounting 32(5–6): 815–870.

Cunningham LA (2013) The Essays of Warren Buffet—Lessons for Corporate America. Carolina Academic Press, Third edition (p 205ff).

Deloitte (2020) Unlocking the Full Potential of M&A—What It Takes to be a Value Creation Champion. ch-en-fa-st-gallen-mergers-acquisitions-study-v2.pdf (http://deloitte.com/).

Draper P, Paudyal K (2006) Acquisitions: Private versus Public. European Financial Management 12(1): 57–80.

Goetz S (2021) Public versus Private: New Insights into the Private Company Discount. Journal of Business Valuation and Economic Loss Analysis.

Graham JR, Harvey CR, Puri M (2013) Managerial Attitudes and Corporate Actions. Journal of Financial Economics 109: 103–121.

Malmendier U, Tate G (2005) CEO Overconfidence and Corporate Investment. The Journal of Finance 60(6): 2661–2700.

McKinsey (2004) Where Mergers Go Wrong. McKinsey on Finance 10: 1–7.

Miles L, Borchert A, Ramanathan AE (2014) Why Some Merging Companies Become Synergy Overachievers. Bain & Company.

Qian J, Lei Zhu J (2018) Return to Invested Capital and the Performance of Mergers Acquisitions. Management Science 64(10): 4818–4834.

Rehm W, Uhlaner R, West A (2012) Taking a Longer-term Look at M&A Value Creation. McKinsey Quarterly.

Renneboog L, Vansteenkiste C (2019) Failure and Success in Mergers and Acquisitions. CentER Discussion Paper Series No. 2019-026.

Chapter 6

BCG (2016) Creating Value Through Active Portfolio Management—The 2016 Value Creators Report.

Bülow S, Mjörnemark NG (2019) The Spinoff Scorecard: An Investment Strategy to Separate the Best Performing Spinoffs from the Worst. Copenhagen Business School.

EY (2019) Will You Set the Divestment Pace, or Try to Keep Up with It? Global Corporate Divestment Study.

Lee DD, Madhavan R (2010) Divestiture and Firm Performance: A Meta-Analysis. Journal of Management 36(6): 1345–1371.

Leimann C (2009) Værdiskabelse gennem frasalg og spaltning: Analyse af Danisco A/S og Novo Nordisk A/S. Institut for Okonomi Arhus Universitet.

Schulman L (2017) How Premium Conglomerates Sustain Success. Published Online. https://www.bcg.com/publications/2017/corporate-strategy-value-creation-premium-conglomerates-sustain-success.

Tjärnström H (2014) Unibet to Propose Distribution of Kambi. Published Online. https://www.kindredgroup.com/media/press-releases/2014/Unibet-to-propose-distribution-of-kambi/.

Chapter 7

Goldman Sachs (2019), Buyback Realities. Published Online. https://www.goldmansachs.com/insights/pages/top-of-mind/buyback-realities/report.pdf.

Chapter 8

Barclay MJ, Smith C (2020) The Capital Structure Puzzle: Another Look at the Evidence. Journal of Applied Corporate Finance 32(1): 80–91.

Harvard Business Review (2003) How Much Cash Does Your Company Need? Published Online. https://hbr.org/2003/11/how-much-cash-does-your-company-need.

Jensen M (1986) Agency Costs of Free Cash Flow; Corporate Finance and Takeovers. American Economic Review 76(2): 323–339.

L'Her, JF, Stoyanova R, Shaw K, Scott W, Lai C (2016) A Bottom-Up Approach to the Risk-Adjusted Performance of the Buyout Fund Market. Financial Analysts Journal 72(4): 1–13.

Chapter 10

Borio C, Disyatat P, Juselius M, Rungcharoenkitkul P (2017) Why So Low for So Long? A Long-term View of Real Interest Rates. BIS Working Papers No. 685.

Buffet WE (1987) Letter to Shareholders, 1987 Berkshire Hathaway Annual Report.

Chapter 11

Barrero JM (2022) The Micro and Macro of Managerial Beliefs. Journal of Financial Economics 143: 640–667.

Credit Suisse (2019) Shareholder Activism: An Evolving Challenge. Published Online. https://www.credit-suisse.com/us/en/investment-banking/ibcm/corporate-insights/shareholder-activism.html.

Goldman Sachs (2023) Do Activist Investors Boost Shareholder Returns? Published Online. https://www.goldmansachs.com/intelligence/pages/do-activist-investors-boost-shareholder-returns.html.

Graham JR, Harvey CR, Puri M (2013) Managerial Attitudes and Corporate Actions. Journal of Financial Economics 109: 103–121.

Kahneman D (2012) Thinking, Fast and Slow. Penguin Books Ltd.

Stotz A, Lu W (2015) Financial Analysts Were Only Wrong by 25%. Published Online. https://papers.ssrn.com/sol3/papers.cfm?abstract_id=2695216.

Thorndike WN (2012) The Outsiders: Eight Unconventional CEOs and Their Radically Rational Blueprint for Success. Harvard Business School Publishing.

Chapter 12

Bain & Company (2019) Beyond the Downturn: Recession Strategies to Take the Lead. Published Online. https://www.bain.com/insights/beyond-the-downturn-recession-strategies-to-take-the-lead/.

BCG (2019) Advantage in Adversity—Winning the Next Downturn. Published Online. https://www.bcg.com/publications/2019/advantage-in-adversity-winning-next-downturn.

Harvard Business Review (2010) Roaring Out of Recession. Published Online. https://hbr.org/2010/03/roaring-out-of-recession.

McKinsey on Finance (2007) Preparing for the Next Downturn. Published Online. https://www.mckinsey.com/capabilities/strategy-and-corporate-finance/our-insights/preparing-for-the-next-downturn.

McKinsey Quarterly (2002) Learning to Love Recessions. Published Online. https://www.inc.com/articles/2002/07/24348.html.

McKinsey Quarterly (2019) Bubbles Pop, Downturns Stop. Published Online. https://www.mckinsey.com/capabilities/strategy-and-corporate-finance/our-insights/bubbles-pop-downturns-stop.

Sandvik (2022) Published Online. https://www.home.sandvik/en/stories/articles/2022/11/resilience-through-agility/.

Chapter 13

Atlas Copco (2016) https://www.atlascopcogroup.com/en/media/corporate-press-releases/2016/20161115-kpis.

Donaldson G (1985) Financial Goals and Strategic Consequences. Harvard Business Review.

Harford J, Kecskés A, and Mansi S (2018) Do Long-Term Investors Improve Corporate Decision Making? Journal of Corporate Finance 50: 424–452.

Novo Nordisk (2022) https://www.novonordisk.com/content/dam/nncorp/global/en/investors/irmaterial/annual_report/2023/novo-nordisk-remuneration-report-2022.pdf.

Stora Enso (2022) https://www.storaenso.com/-/media/documents/download-center/documents/annual-reports/2022/storaenso_annual_report_2022.pdf#page=116.

Appendix

Mauboussin MJ, Callahan D (2022) Return on Invested Capital: How to Calculate ROIC and Handle Common Issues. Published Online. https://www.morganstanley.com/im/publication/insights/articles/article_returnoninvestedcapital.pdf.

Index

T. Arenbo, *Capital Allocation and Value Creation*,
https://doi.org/10.1007/978-3-031-47048-6

GPSR Compliance
The European Union's (EU) General Product Safety Regulation (GPSR) is a set of rules that requires consumer products to be safe and our obligations to ensure this.

If you have any concerns about our products, you can contact us on

ProductSafety@springernature.com

In case Publisher is established outside the EU, the EU authorized representative is:

Springer Nature Customer Service Center GmbH
Europaplatz 3
69115 Heidelberg, Germany

www.ingramcontent.com/pod-product-compliance
Lightning Source LLC
Chambersburg PA
CBHW051602220626
47054CB00004B/114
9783031470479